TALES
OUT OF SCHOOL

BOOKS BY GEOFFREY TREASE

Books for Young Readers

No Boats on Bannermere

Black Banner Players

The Gates of Bannerdale

Seven Kings of England

The Maythorn Story

Bows Against the Barons

Cue for Treason

The Grey Adventurer

The Silken Secret

The Hills of Varna

The Crown of Violet

Mist Over Athelney

Follow My Black Plume

The Young Traveller in England and Wales

The Young Traveller in India and Pakistan

The Young Traveller in Greece

Under Black Banner

Black Banner Abroad

The Seven Queens of England

Seven Stages

Change at Maythorn

In the Land of the Mogul

Silver Guard

Trumpets in the West

The Barons' Hostage

The Secret Fiord

Word to Caesar

Thunder of Valmy

Fortune My Foe

Enjoying Books

The Young Writer

Novels

Snared Nightingale

So Wild the Heart

History

The Italian Story

TALES
OUT OF SCHOOL

by

GEOFFREY TREASE

SECOND EDITION

Ficta voluptatis causa sint proxima veris
HORACE

HEINEMANN EDUCATIONAL
BOOKS LTD · LONDON

Heinemann Educational Books Ltd
LONDON MELBOURNE TORONTO
SINGAPORE CAPE TOWN
AUCKLAND IBADAN
HONG KONG

SECOND EDITION © Geoffrey Trease 1964
FIRST PUBLISHED 1949
REPRINTED 1949
SECOND EDITION 1964
REPRINTED 1965

Published by
Heinemann Educational Books Ltd
48 Charles Street, London W1
Printed in Great Britain
by Bookprint Limited
Kingswood, Surrey

In memory of
My Father,
who loved
a good yarn.

CONTENTS

Preface to the Second Edition   ix

I   How Much Does it Matter?   1

II   Myself When Young   17

III   Looking at the Pictures   30

IV   Fancy Free   40

V   The Fringe of Fact   53

VI   The Comic and the Blood   64

VII   Tough as They Come   77

VIII   Cloak and Sword   95

IX   Midnight in the Dorm   107

X   The Family in Fiction   124

XI   Home and Holiday   138

XII   To You – For Action   156

Bibliography   171

Index   173

ILLUSTRATIONS

The illustrations have been <u>selected</u> as examples of the variety of pictures to be found in the children's literature discussed in this book. For permission to reproduce these, grateful acknowledgements are due to the sources given.

Edward Ardizzone: from *The Otterbury Incident* by C. Day Lewis (Pitman) 15

From the strip 'Fidosaurus, the Prehistoric Poodle' in *Eagle*, June 1963 (Odhams Press) 29

Kathleen Gell: from *Come In* by Olive Dehn (Shakespeare Head Press) 33

Joan Kiddell-Monroe: from *The Odyssey of Homer* by Leonie Picard (Oxford University Press) 38

Robert Gibbings: from *The Insect Man* by Eleanor Doorly (Heinemann) 60

Lance Cattermole: from *Sail Ho!* by Shalimar (Oxford University Press) 90

William Stobbs: from *Nicholas Carey* by Ronald Welch (Oxford University Press) 103

Isabel Veevers: from *The House on the Cliffs* by Rita Coatts (Evan Brothers) 109

From the strip 'Billy Binns' in *Boys' World*, February 1964 (Odhams Press) 112

Jack Matthews: from *Feud in the Factory* by Lorna Lewis (Oxford University Press) 135

David Knight: from *Songberd's Grove* by Anne Barrett (Collins) 147

Preface to the Second Edition

THE demand for a new edition comes to any author as something of a compliment. When it involves drastic revision – and when he is primarily an imaginative writer, keener to explore new territory than to retrace his steps – it can be also something of a chore. In the present instance it would be ungracious indeed to complain, since such a happy reason compels the rewriting of so many passages. The fifteen years following the original publication of this little book have seen great advances in children's literature and no one could be more delighted than its author if they have rendered some of his jeremiads obsolete.

At the same time there is evidence that many grounds for criticism remain. Plenty of trash is still being published – and in any case the bookshelves are not cleared and refilled each season. Children are still reading the books, good, bad or mediocre, published long before this volume itself appeared. Indeed, in the libraries of some expensive private schools they are offered little else. For that reason, though the chance has been welcomed to insert many new names and titles, there has been no move to jettison every book just because it has declined in popularity with the years. A book has not finished its work when the bookseller can no longer supply a new copy. It goes on, and sooner or later, if it has the stuff of immortality in it, public demand will quietly build up and make its re-issue feasible. If 'out of print' came to mean 'unmentionable', many a good book would never be rescued from the limbo into which it had temporarily fallen.

Nor has this present revision, while attempting to bring the survey up to date, been designed to be comprehensive – it remains what it confessed itself to be originally, 'a personal survey of general tendencies as they are discoverable by a single critic'. Since those words were written there has been so much admirable work by Kathleen Lines, Margery Fisher, and others, that it would be even more pointless than before to essay that kind of task here.

Colwall, 1964   G.T.

CHAPTER ONE

How Much Does it Matter?

AS a boy I was strongly discouraged from wasting my twopences on the detective adventures of Sexton Blake, and, if I brought Buffalo Bill into the house, no Cherokee could have been prompter than my father to pounce upon him. The distinction is more important than apparent. My father liked Buffalo Bill . . .

This, I think, was the only deliberate influence exercised at home upon my embryonic literary taste, and the only suggestion that parents had a responsibility in the matter. Already, all those years ago, there was a weakening in that deep moral conviction which had sustained parents and schoolmasters for a couple of centuries: that it mattered what children read in their leisure-time, and mattered very much indeed; that 'tales out of school' were as potent an influence as lessons inside.

'*Cinderella*,' wrote a lady in 1802, 'is perhaps one of the most exceptionable books that was ever written for children. It paints some of the worst passions that can enter into the human breast – envy, jealousy, vanity, a love of dress.' No doubt she was somewhat mollified when *Cinderella*, later in the century, was re-written as temperance propaganda, and the wedding scene culminated in a grand bonfire of all the alcohol in the royal cellars. She disapproved just as much of *Robinson Crusoe*, which, she feared, might lead 'to an early taste for a rambling life and a love of adventure'.

'There is not a species of Books for Children and Youth,' agreed Sarah Trimmer in her *Essay on Christian Education*, 'which has not been made in some way or other an engine of mischief.' Maria Hack, in 1821, gloomily reduced story-books to the same level as the least mentionable of excesses. 'It may be doubted,' she remarks without a hint of doubt in her voice, 'whether habituating children to seek amusement, almost exclusively, in fictitious narrative, has not a direct tendency to weaken the natural powers.'

The trade, to do it justice, strove hard to meet these objections. The moral content of books was guaranteed as though it were Vitamin C. James Catnach, the early-nineteenth-century bookseller and publisher of chap-books, advertised his shop in Seven Dials with the rhyme:

> Little Boys and Girls will find
> At Catnach's something to their mind,
> From great variety may choose
> What will instruct them and amuse . . .
> Instruction unto youth when given
> Points the path from earth to heaven.
> He sells by Wholesale and Retail,
> To suit all moral tastes can't fail.

Authors co-operated. Sarah Trimmer herself, in a footnote to her *Fabulous Histories*, pointed out: 'A mockbird is properly a native of America, but is introduced here for the sake of the moral.'

Few adults doubted that these moral injections were essential to spiritual health. Parents in those days might not call their children 'little devils' as freely as we do, but they were far more deeply convinced that this was precisely what they were. 'All children are by nature evil,' said Mrs Sherwood, creator of *The Fairchild Family*. There seemed only one point worthy of discussion – did fiction make them better or worse?

We have now had more than two centuries of children's literature, produced as such, and distinct from adult books like *Robinson Crusoe* and *Gulliver's Travels*, which have only accidentally found their immortality in the nursery. Children's literature may be dated from *A Little Pretty Pocket Book*, published (and probably written) by John Newbery in 1744; story-books came in 1761 with *Goody Two-shoes*. If Goldsmith really wrote that, as many believe, he was the first of the long line of English authors, stretching down to Walter de la Mare and Cecil Day Lewis in our own time, who have not allowed their main work for adults to prevent their contributing to the juvenile shelves.

For the first of those two centuries the terrible twins, Morality and Instruction, stalk arrogantly through almost every story. They are its *raison d'être*. All else is incidental. When Thomas Day wrote *Sandford and Merton* it was because he wanted to popularize Rousseau's philosophy in English. 'To render the relation more interesting to those for whom it was intended, I have introduced two children as the actors,' he wrote graciously. Could concession and compromise go further? No nonsense about giving the kiddies what they loved. As soon would the family doctor have produced peppermints instead of pills. For fifty years after *Sandford and Merton*, says F. J. Harvey Darton in that delicious and invaluable historical survey, *Children's Books in England*, 'neither writers nor readers expected anything but didacticism'.

By the mid-nineteenth century a new attitude began to show itself. It was still unquestioned that the content of children's books mattered very much. But the terrible twins had been with us rather a long time; they were getting too old to walk about naked. So, with good scriptural authority, they learnt to hide behind trees, popping out only when the young reader's interest was securely snared by a dramatic situation; or they camouflaged themselves so effectively in the dress of castaways, fur-traders, or boys of Rugby School, that they were accepted gladly and without suspicion.

It is very easy to poke fun at the piety of the first phase and at the 'manliness' cult of the second, but in fairness the authors should be judged against the background of their times. What were these morals they wished to teach? Kindness to animals was one. If we think ourselves back for a moment into the brutal atmosphere of the late eighteenth century (and later), to the bull-baitings, cock-fights, and other organized horrors, not to mention the impromptu sadism of small boys with cats and dogs, we may feel that it was not so funny. We may feel, too, that the pious story, in denouncing these things, played an honourable part in the gradual transformation of public opinion. If not, what did? People, as we are frequently reminded, are not changed by Act of Parliament alone. Anti-slavery was another theme for the moralist, when slavery was a world-wide reality. If we permit ourselves a superior smile at all, it had better not be at the morals but at the way in which they were conveyed. Which, of course, is about as sensible as patronizing Henry Fielding because he had not developed the technique of Henry James.

So too the ideal of 'Christian manliness' was not without value in its time. It is easy to guy. *With Bible and Bayonet* may not be an authentic title, but one feels a little surprised that it was never used by any writer of the Henty school. The French Academician, Paul Hazard, poked fun at this genre in his *Books, Children and Men* – gentle fun, because he loved the 'fortunate isle of books for young people'. 'England,' he says, 'could be reconstructed entirely from its children's books. We learn at once from them that John Bull was never ashamed to say his prayers . . .' And again, they 'encourage a taste for sport, and exalt, not the individual triumph, but the victory of the team . . . Learn, children, to love the sailor's life, set sail in your thoughts, travel over the seas in quest of adventure and danger. Above all, never be afraid. See how the English pull through by means of courage and calm, in shipwrecks and fires, in expeditions against pirates and cannibals, in the land of the yellow or black man. Lost in the desert, prisoners, and already bound to the stake, see, they do not tremble . . .' Children's fiction no more built the British Empire than it abolished, single-handed, slavery and cruelty to animals, but its indirect influence was not trivial. Did the imperialists of those days consciously desire, through adventure stories, to 'encourage the growth of an adventurously-minded generation which believed it had a world of great possibilities before it'? Who can say? For that last quotation is not from Paul Hazard but from George Reavey's *Soviet Literature Today*. In Russia they are sufficiently old-fashioned to be concerned with what their children read.

We have finished with all that in the free and enlightened West. To suggest any control or direction of children's reading produces shocked reaction. What are control and direction but censorship? Let the child range freely. He is omnivorous. What he does not understand will not hurt him: what he understands, he is ready for. Trash does not harm, only by his own selection and rejection can he acquire the genuine standards of taste which alone are worth while . . .

Stop. I too can go on like that for several pages. I too can evoke nostalgic pictures of the old study at home, with Father, unusually enlightened for his generation, steadying the step-ladder while my youthful fingers draw the *Decameron* from the top shelf. The picture is imaginary, for we had no study at home, but it is quite true that I cut my teeth on Sax Rohmer and Pope's *Iliad* with equal relish. Fine! (We slap our chests at this point.) It never did *us* any harm, did it? No, but . . . that remark has a familiar ring. Are we conceivably echoing those Old Boys who defend corporal punishment?

This is no plea for prohibition of any kind. The 'free range' is the ideal. But is it at present possible in the average home? Surely the picture of the well-stocked study is sentimental and unreal. It is true for the daughters of dons and for some hundreds of thousands of others who read the weekly reviews – real perhaps for you, who have read this book so far. But let your mind's eye, like a cinema-camera, pan across the anonymous roof-tops of the Corporation housing estate, and then focus and track down into a single interior. What are the chances of a well-stocked bookcase, let alone a study? Even the unread rows of Scott and Dickens and Thackeray, which graced the sitting-room in earlier generations, have probably gone to make room for the television set. One hears of miners who have lovingly collected libraries of a thousand volumes or more, and crammed them into their small cottages. But these are untypical. Very, very few modern homes, whatever the income-group of the householder, offer even a good mixture of adult and children's books.

There are the libraries. Exactly. There is a good deal to be said on that point. I have been inside scores of children's libraries up and down England: no doubt I have seen the best, for my visits have been mainly connected with Book Weeks, which are seldom held by lazy librarians and may be impossible (because of inadequate premises) for some of the keen ones. I have seen enough to make me wistful about my own childhood, when I was not allowed to visit the dark and depressing public library for fear of germs and dirt. I envy the new generation these airy rooms with gay friezes, light oak furniture, and clean new books. The best of the British libraries are now magnificent. Yet do they offer a completely free range? Of course not. Except for some border-line authors like John Buchan and Marjorie Bowen, adult books are usually shelved in another department requiring separate tickets. Apart from the possible fury of some ratepayers if they found their children bringing home *Tropic of Cancer* from the junior department, any public library is compelled to divide its stock in a way which limits the actual, even more than the potential, range of its younger borrowers. School libraries must be still more selective. Funds and facilities are more limited, and they are, if anything, more vulnerable to parental criticism. 'One black ball excludes.' One shockable parent – who may not exist, but on the other hand may – is enough to keep out a book which, while possessing many positive virtues, may seem to infringe one of the established political, national or religious taboos.

Selection, whether deliberate or accidental, is thus inevitable in both public and private libraries. The picture of the child browsing in the book-walled room, with the firelight playing softly on the handsome bindings and a bust of Voltaire beaming down as he collects a mixed armful of Hans Andersen and Havelock Ellis, belongs to the age of a leisured middle-class minority, when books, both adult and juvenile, were few enough for a cultured family to maintain a representative collection. Now we have the paradox of too many children's books (in the shops) and too few (in the home). Fresh titles are spawned like herrings every season. Dorothy Neal White, the New Zealand librarian, says in her witty and knowledgeable *About Books for Children* that the average child, between its seventh and its fourteenth birthdays, reads only about four hundred books. Enid Blyton, perhaps the most prolific English author for younger children, can write ten thousand words per day, supplies sixteen different publishers, and has to date produced several hundred books. She is a phenomenon, but there are others who can hardly be dismissed as sterile – Captain W. E. Johns has written some dozens of his 'Biggles' stories alone. The case for selection hardly needs arguing further.

Mrs White selected. In her library at Dunedin she 'steadily withdrew the second-rate books . . . Nothing was bought unless it had some literary merit and some originality, unless it was a contribution to modern children's literature. It might have been expected that while the standard of books issued would improve appreciably the number circulated might conceivably have fallen. The reverse was the case. As the quality of our stock improved, the quantity we were able to issue increased. Children had confirmed our trust in their good taste. The range of good children's books is somewhere under 5,000 titles; this offers any child a wide choice in selecting his 400-odd books between seven and fourteen years.' It is fair to add that both her figures have been disputed. A London librarian, Miss Eileen H. Colwell, thinks the average is nearer 600 than 400, but wonders 'also whether it is possible to find as many as 5,000 titles of a really good standard for children, even including American books as well as English'.

That is a new thought. Too few? Too few 'good' ones. It depends what you mean by a good children's book. Let's face that now. The question will recur in every chapter, but let's fight the first round.

In the old days it would have been quite easy. The book was subjected to a series of tests. Did it contain bad grammar or slang? Blasphemy and foul language could be indicated, but not of course quoted, by the phrase 'drunken oaths', with which the villains went about their work. It was implied that even villains would not so far forget themselves unless under the influence of alcohol. (The consumption of alcohol was, incidentally, restricted to villains, and permitted to heroes only when the action took place prior to 1837.) Stories must have a healthy tone: there could be unlimited bloodshed and sadistic torture but no hint of affection between the sexes. They must be patriotic. They must be imbued with Christian morality of an evangelical type: cracks at the Catholic Church were quite safe, and often encouraged. There was, finally, the question of whether the book would entertain the child, but this was rhetorical. Without public libraries, cinemas and broadcasting, the child had little choice. Even nowadays, when driven into a corner by circumstances, most children will enjoy almost anything.

It was good that adult arrogance should take a fall. To claim now that you know what is good for a child is to bring the derision of every adult upon your head. Not wishing to be dubbed a pompous prig, you don't say it. You may wonder why doctors and nurses and mothers are not similarly howled down when they prescribe bedtimes, orange-juice, sea air or remedial exercises for flat feet. Why don't we shout at them: 'What do *you* know about it ? You – whose own childhood is twenty, thirty, forty years behind you – how dare you presume to say what is needed for modern children ?' Can it be because, while we have kept a little faith in medical men and mothers, we have none left in morality ? That we dare not claim to know what is good for the child because we are no longer certain what is good for ourselves ?

It is a fashionable proposition that 'only children know what other children like'. It was some of the intellectual weeklies which began the regrettable practice of allowing the scant space allotted to children's book-reviews to be filled by juvenile contributors. Master Tommy Tucker (aged 7) signs a mono-syllabic appreciation of a new animal story, and Janet Jodhpur (aged 12) deals breezily with the latest thing in holiday mysteries. An actual review by a thirteen-year-old boy in *Time and Tide* ran: 'This is a very good book, it is very well written . . . This book is worth reading and I advise all boys and girls from 7 to 13 to read it . . . I enjoyed it very much and so will all others who read it.' Now this is all very kind, if a little repetitive, but it is not criticism. (I have omitted only a few sentences, which contained nothing but a muddled resumé of the plot.) It is always very warming to be liked, but the function of *Time and Tide* is not to warm me, or any other author. It is to tell us, through competent judges of style and content, whether we are writing well or badly.

All this mystery about 'what children like' is just part of the modern myth that all children are angels of instinctive wisdom and all adults are blundering, pompous fools. It is not hard to discover what children like. Most teachers can give you a rough idea in five minutes' conversation. Any children's librarian can give you a fair general picture in ten. There are published results of scientific surveys, like A. J. Jenkinson's *What Do Boys and Girls Read?*

It is generally assumed – I cannot think why – that the best book is the one most children like. 'There is only one criterion,' Captain Johns told me, 'and that is the number that it sells.' We do not apply this standard to adult literature or any other art; if we did, we should hear some strange music played in the Albert Hall and see some unexpected pictures hung in the Tate. Every other art has its standards independent of box-office returns. May not ours?

In his *Manual of Children's Libraries* W. C. Berwick Sayers attempted to lay down such standards. A book, he said, must have literary style, or at least good English. It must have 'wholesome imagination' and 'a right sense of wit and humour'. It must be 'true' and 'law-abiding'. All these terms call for long definition before they can carry us much further. Having written thus far, I realize I am out on a limb, and cannot avoid a tentative definition of my own. I see only one distinction between a good children's book and any other good book – which is that its theme and vocabulary must be within the grasp of the young. But, there being no agreed definition of a good book, I cannot escape that way. So, with all deference, I submit this: 'A good children's book is one which uses language skilfully to entertain and to represent reality, to stimulate the imagination or to educate the emotions.' Entertainment is essential. Children may like a bad book, but a book none of them likes cannot be good. Entertainment is so easy to provide that it is not unreasonable to expect at least one of the other three desiderata. I assume that these *are* desirable things, because they seem to be among the objects of the general educational system we all pay for, and – provided always that in stories the genuine entertainment comes first – it is common sense that writers and educationists should work together rather than at cross-purposes.

'If we believe whole-heartedly in books,' says Eleanor Graham, 'we must recognize more than mere entertainment as their function, important as that is.' And Malcolm Saville, whose popularity with children is unquestionable, says: 'we, who write for the men and women of tomorrow, have great responsibilities and must recognize them.' Yet the contemporary prejudice dies hard, that the children's writer with a conscious purpose must necessarily be a bore and a prig. Other writers are acclaimed if they have something to say, but not those who write for the young.

In fact, of course, neither Miss Graham nor Mr Saville is pilloried as a bore or a prig, because most adults know their names only by hearsay, as authors of books their children have probably enjoyed. Few adults will have read those books and even fewer will have seen the specialized journals (*Junior Bookshelf* and *The Author* respectively) in which these statements appeared. Adults do not normally read children's books. It would be unnatural if they did. Years ago, if a friend mentioned one to me, assuming that I should know all about it, I felt mildly irritated. 'My dear chap,' I would say, 'I *write* children's books – I don't read them.' This was not arrogance, but a normal adult reaction, reinforced in my own case by a fear that I might fall unconsciously into plagiarism.

There came, however, a period of years when I reviewed large numbers of new children's books and when the flow of these through the house was supplemented by the older volumes then being borrowed and devoured by a bibliophil daughter. I was made aware, willy-nilly, of what other people were writing.

When a brief radio talk led, unexpectedly, to the commissioning of this survey, I became aware how much leeway I had to make up, if I were to back my impressions and prejudices with the kind of evidence that would make them worth airing. This is a whole field of literature, of which few but professional and school librarians can claim a comprehensive knowledge. No creative writer should have the time to spend seeking such knowledge – he must make his own distinctive contribution to the discussion on another level. When I first undertook this survey I read and looked at children's books innumerable. I followed up the recommendations of children, librarians, teachers, and others. But as every research-worker knows, there comes a time when one must cry halt and get down to the arrangement of one's material. I wrote then, still daunted after the contemplation of so many books: 'I shudder to think of the thousands I have not seen, and of the good authors I may neglect to mention. But this book is a personal survey of general tendencies as they are discoverable by a single critic, with all the limitations of time and mortality'. Fifteen years later, despite much subsequent reading and all the helpful suggestions and corrections gratefully accepted from correspondents, lecture-hall questioners and others, those words must stand.

What adults know about this subject is nearly always out of date. Amiable aunts tend to give as presents the books which they enjoyed themselves in that improbable youth they must once have experienced. They also give books which are too 'young' for their respectful but wry-faced recipients, partly because aunts seldom realize how quickly their nieces and nephews are growing up, and partly because, with the progressive sophistication of modern children, what once suited the sixteen-year-old is now outgrown at fourteen or earlier.

Parents do occasionally read children's books, mainly from selfish motives. More than one boy has told me how strict fathers can be about bed-time when they want to get their fingers on the latest volume from the junior library. This is understandable in a period when, crime-thrillers excepted, the novel has so largely abandoned action and plot for depressing psychological studies of failure and frustration. Mothers seem to examine their children's books with less selfish ends. An article in *Housewife* entitled 'Books and Your Child' brought a whole crop of letters which revealed first-hand knowledge and a genuine, if sometimes rather blindly-groping, concern.

Librarians read children's books a good deal. Reviewers ... well, dog does not eat dog, so we will say little, except that large numbers of books do not need to be read to be 'noticed' – a flick of the pages or a glance down the chapter headings is enough. Twins, a secret passage, a hooded figure, smugglers, stolen jewels ... Unfortunately the books have to be mentioned, if not read, and so little space is left for those books which possess a spark of originality that it is hardly worth reading them either, except for one's own pleasure. This question of criticism will recur later on.

What about teachers? Surely they read children's books, or at least those which are potential aids to their work? Surely they will salute as allies those authors who, braving the stigma of 'educational value', toil to bring History to life, to transport young readers vividly into those very lands which occupied last week's Geography lesson, or to awaken their imagination to the potentialities of Science? Alas, no. 'I am totally ignorant of modern children's fiction,' a schoolmaster wrote to me. He was History specialist in a well-known boarding-school. It had not occurred to him that after, say, a painstaking class-room explanation that nationalism did not originate before the late Middle Ages, a boy might go out and read an enthralling yarn of the Norman Conquest in which a Saxon leader, somewhat confusingly saluting his crew as 'sea-cocks', assured them in the true Nelson spirit that 'one Englishman is a match for two Frenchmen'. The schoolmaster may of course retort, what does it matter? It does not matter; if he cares nothing about teaching history, or alternatively if he feels he can safely assume that his abstract, class-room presentation of the idea is so potent that it can obliterate the contradictory idea portrayed in a gripping adventure story. The profession has its share of cynicism and conceit, but it is probably fairer to say that most teachers are ignorant of their pupils' leisure-reading because they feel too busy to investigate and have little idea of what they would find if they did.

Having taught a little, I sympathize. 'Have a heart!' I hear some mistress say. 'I have had a nerve-jangling day in the classroom, a strenuous afternoon on the hockey field, a row with a colleague and an exasperating five minutes with the Head. Now, having waded through that pile of exercise books, I am expected – this not being a night I have an evening class to take – to spend my last waking hours reading *A Pony for Penelope* or *Mystery at St. Monica's*. Well, I'm damned well not going to. I'm going to switch on the radio and pick up the paper – and, mark you, for the first time today!'

Not every day is quite so full for every teacher, but there are other claims on her leisure which we have not mentioned. Let us consider only reading, leaving aside all other responsibilities and recreations. Of course she must read the paper: she will be lacking as teacher if she knows nothing of current affairs. She may feel too that, spending so much of her day in immature society, she ought to get her teeth into some really adult book – fiction or otherwise – if she is not to suffer that intellectual deterioration which becomes an increasing occupational risk as the year of graduation recedes. Finally, supposing for the sake of argument that she too is a History specialist, she may feel it more important to keep abreast of new developments in her own subject by reading academic reviews than by following the adventures of Sir Ralph Ruddiblade across the Spanish Main.

The amazing thing is that any teacher reads any juvenile books at all. They not only do, they write them, eminent examples being the late Eleanor Doorly, headmistress of Warwick High School, Ian Serraillier and Henry Treece. Those teachers who realize the potentialities of juvenile fiction seem to manage somehow to keep in touch with it. But these teachers are few and far between. Too many of the profession know nothing about the books their pupils read outside. Much is being attempted now to improve matters, by lectures in training colleges and at refresher courses, and by the arrangement of book-exhibitions.

This chapter has gone on quite long enough. I have tried to show that until modern times no one questioned the importance of what children read, but that now, as part of the general reaction against the moralists, it is consciously admitted by very few. Entertainment is assumed to be the sole, rather than merely the first, aim of children's stories; from which it follows that the children, being indisputably the soundest judges of their own entertainment, need no benevolent influence upon their selection. A minority of parents and adults dissent.

'We can disregard the literature for childhood only if we consider unimportant the way in which a national soul is formed and sustained,' wrote the Frenchman, Paul Hazard. 'Boys' fiction,' said the English George Orwell in 1940, 'is sodden in the worst illusions of 1910. The fact is only unimportant if one believes that what is read in childhood leaves no impression behind.'

In 1963 the Bishop of London was confessing to the House of Lords that after fifty years he had still not got G. A. Henty quite out of his system, and the Borough Librarian of St Pancras was banning Biggles because 'his attitude to coloured people reflects an outmoded Kipling approach, which many people these days consider bad for children'. The creator of Biggles, Captain W. E. Johns, promptly answered this by quoting Graham Greene (*Sunday Times*, 1953) that in Kenya 'a missionary told me that the works of Shakespeare and the Biggles books were the only forms of imaginative literature to which he had found his pupils attracted'. This remark invites more fascinating questions than can be considered here. One wonders what these African children would have made of *The Rolling Season* by William Mayne, a distinguished (if sometimes difficult) writer of the newer school, who in this realistic Wiltshire story includes a West Indian bus conductor among his characters.

Let us conclude with the comments of two London school-mistresses. '*Rupert's Annual*,' they write, 'is a favourite with the younger children. Among the characters is Tiger Lily, daughter

of a Chinese conjuror. She is presented as a typical Chinese girl, and the children whom we questioned seemed to think she was meant to be a figure of fun. They told us that in earlier volumes Rupert had visited other countries where there were some very funny people.' Nationalism, of course, is only one facet of the problem. They continue: 'We find the general trend of their reading encourages the attitude that children know better than adults, that all foreigners are uncivilized and peculiar, that all history took place at some vague unspecified date called "the olden days", and that a book is not interesting unless it provides exciting and improbable incidents on every page.'

It is comforting to feel that even if we are cranks to think it matters, at least we are not isolated cranks.

CHAPTER TWO

Myself When Young

WE stir pools deeper than we realize when we start a discussion on children's reading. We have known only one childhood, our own, and the books we loved then come leaping back to our memory like so many splendid, glittering salmon. How much better we remember them, once they are called back to mind, than the hundreds of adult novels which have filled the intervening years! 'Never,' wrote Sir Herbert Read in *The Innocent Eye*, 'have I known such absorption and excitement as gripped me when I first read *King Solomon's Mines*.' And how much more emotional is our defence of those bygone favourites than of even the most 'important' adult fiction. . . . We can discuss without heat the work of Proust and Virginia Woolf, but if a carping voice is raised against E. Nesbit or Ballantyne or Henty or whoever was our childhood love, then the fat is quickly in the fire.

It is important to recognize this. However ably we study the child of today, his altered interests and enlarged general know-ledge, it is the child of yesterday – our inescapable selves – who will mould our opinion. The bias and prejudices which are unavoidable in any one-man survey like this go far back beyond the years of writing and teaching, reviewing and lecturing in libraries: they spring from the books which that one man read when young. So with the individual reader. The worst irritation provoked (and, with the best will in the world, dare he hope to escape provoking irritation?) will rise from the difference between *his* favourites and those of each separate reader.

Glancing at my own list you may cry instinctively: 'Alice, where art thou?' *Alice in Wonderland* (from which, by contrast, Sir Hugh Walpole learnt to read) was introduced to me by a scandalized schoolmaster when I was thirteen and starting

Greek. Of *The Wind in the Willows* I remained unconscious until, as a Sixth Former, I read of it in an essay by A. A. Milne, and sought it out. I say this with regret but without shame. A child can read only those books he finds to hand, a fact which is no less tremendously important because it sounds obvious.

What was to hand? There were little fairy-stories at the back of – was it *Home Notes*? They were all the same – a little girl going to bed, waking to find a fairy-coach on the window-sill, undergoing a rapid reducing process, driving off to Queen Mab's court and waking up in the morning to be assured, against all her own convictions, that it had been 'only a dream'. There was Teddy Tail of the *Daily Mail* . . . I can still see that adorable mouse wading pathetically across the endless morass of a treacle-tart. There were Aladdin, Ali Baba and Sinbad. There were the weeklies, *Puck* and *Rainbow* and *The Jester*. Later there was the *Children's Newspaper* from its first issue – it had serials in those days, and I vividly remember the first one about an air exploration of the Sargasso Sea. Arthur Mee, its founder, despised fiction. 'I have never bothered about fairy-tales or fiction,' he is quoted as saying in G. J. H. Northcroft's manual, *Writing for Children*. 'I certainly think that except for very little people there is little chance for fairy-tales today. I should say they are the things to begin a child's interest with and to drop as soon as the child begins to take an interest in the things about him. I am personally sorry for anybody who must have stories invented for him in a world like this.' Yet there is perhaps more – even in 'a world like this' – than can be compressed within the covers of his *Children's Encyclopaedia*.

Being the youngest in a family of boys, I naturally turned early to adventure stories. I knew every inch of *The Coral Island* and of that more sterile strand where the *Red Eric* was cast away. *Treasure Island* I found as a serial in an old bound volume of the weekly, *Chums*. *Robinson Crusoe* we had in a short version, and *The Swiss Family* in full. A curious book, that. Persistently pious, indigestibly didactic, it should logically have died long ago. Yet Alison Uttley says she read it seven times in succession, and even today it holds many a youthful reader. William Godwin was translating it in 1814 in those very months when Shelley was planning his elopement with Mary, and it has been suggested that the poet lent a hand. Young men will certainly perform the most unlikely services in the home of the girl they desire.

My interests were not confined to islands. I ranged the Congo with *The Gorilla-Hunters* and the Brazilian jungle with *Martin Rattler*. I trekked *North Overland with Franklin*. At Henty's call I marched *With Roberts to Pretoria, With the Allies to Pekin, With Kitchener in the Sudan* and, I suppose, with almost every military expedition from Hannibal and his elephants onwards. I loved, too, the factual accounts of Cook's voyages and Livingstone's journeys, Alfred in Athelney and Hereward in the Fens, the mutiny of the *Bounty* and the march of the Ten Thousand. My only library facilities were a single shelf in the Mechanics' Institution, whence, using my father's ticket, I could borrow those well-thumbed volumes of *Chums,* the *B.O.P.,* and the *Captain*. So I was driven to tackle whatever printed matter there was in the house – the six volumes of the encyclopaedia, the bound copies of the *Illustrated London News* covering the years of the Crimean and Franco-Prussian Wars and anything else I could lay hands on.

These are the books which leap first to memory. Only after them come the school-stories, *Eric* and *St. Winifred's* and *The Hill* and *The Cock House at Fellsgarth*; and the scientific romances of Jules Verne. There is a significant connection between what I read then and what I have written since. It is emphasized by the fact that my greatest favourite of all was a *Chums* serial, A. S. Walkey's *Hurrah for Merry Sherwood!* and that the first boys' story I wrote was called *Bows Against the Barons*.

'How long have you been writing stories?' people sometimes ask. In a sense since before I knew my ABC. I used to sit quiet in a corner at a small table chequered for draughts, scribbling in old ledgers and desk-diaries page after page of meaningless arabesques, while muttering under my breath the story I was inventing but could not transcribe. Later, when I could write, others unfortunately could read, and my notebooks had to be pushed far back beneath the sofa to save them from curious eyes. I still remember the laughter when my brother declaimed the opening lines of my shipwreck story: '*Crash! The captain's head struck the deck* . . .' I forget now why it struck the deck – whether the immediate cause was the shock of the vessel against a coral reef or a belaying-pin wielded by a mutineer – but I feel now it was a better opening than I dared to think then. The young reader would go on, because he would wonder why. I still do myself, but unless my unconscious releases some more of the story I shall never know.

At eleven I was editing a form magazine running five serials from one term to the next. (Always the emphasis on fiction, in spite of Arthur Mee.) At thirteen, offered the choice of a bicycle or a cricket-bat, I deeply disturbed my father by begging for a second-hand typewriter. With characteristic magnanimity he let the unnatural child have his way. . . . I was sent out with his clerk to find a solid old Remington, and soon I was producing, in a rich purple type with water-colour illustrations, *The British Boys' Magazine*, 'published exclusively by the proprietor: R. G. Trease', and lent to subscribers at a halfpenny a day. Before me as I write is a rare surviving issue, No. 6, Vol. II. Its tone is aggressively patriotic. It announces as a forthcoming attraction 'another fine story of The League of Imperialists'. It contains an African serial, *Fighting the Slavers*, derived from Dr Gordon Stables' *Adventures of Harry Milvaine*, a short story, *Fernstone's Field-Day*, in which O.T.C. cadets deal effectively with 'rioters' who assail 'the ivy-covered mansion' of a local industrialist, and the usual South American story in which the young Britisher settles the internal upsets of a miniature republic. It is again significant, perhaps, that my third published book was laid in a similar republic, though by then I was drawing my inspiration from the Gran Chaco and the facts revealed by the League of Nations inquiry into the private armaments traffic. I had abandoned my benevolent young Britisher, along with that mysterious señorita, with 'dark, lustrous eyes', who figures in the earlier tale. She was, she told young Harry, ' "in a dilemma. If I leave the palace I may be caught again by Rodrigo. But to stop here – oh! It is unthinkable, impossible!" And she shuddered as if gripped by some nameless fear.' Why did Rodrigo want to catch her? Juanita's dilemma must remain another of those tantalizing literary losses.

My determination to write never failed. I remember being asked, by that same stern Greek master who had thundered at me because I knew not Alice: 'And what are *you* going to be?' I answered timidly that I hoped to write; I think I used the phrase 'literary work'. He pressed me for greater definition. 'I – I thought of starting as a reporter,' I floundered, trying to make my dream sound practicable, and he roared with laughter because I saw no contradiction.

I had never the slightest intention of becoming a children's writer. Year by year I poured out poems, essays, plays. . . . At twenty I was selling guinea articles to small papers and hawking an unpublishable novel round Bloomsbury and Covent Garden. At twenty-four, all boats burnt, I was trying every market from women's magazines to literary reviews. I had, some time previously, come across Ilin's documentary children's book, *Moscow Has a Plan*. The idea germinated slowly, and one day burst suddenly forth, that children's books were not reflecting the changed values of the age. Adult fiction was. Novelists in the nineteen-thirties did not depict war as glorious or the British as a superior race. Children's books had kept the pre-1914 outlook. There must be many 'progressive parents' (blessed phrase) who had acquired children somehow, in spite of the current vogue for contraception and abortion, and who felt uneasy at putting them to bed with Herbert Strang or Percy Westerman while they went off to a meeting of the I.L.P. or the League Against Imperialism. I wrote to a publisher whose list indicated probable sympathy, and suggested several ideas, one being a realistic Robin Hood story, in which the seamy side of Merrie England should be displayed, and Robin represented as a kind of premature Wat Tyler. (Much later I was interested to find that Walter Ralegh, when on trial for his life, took the same view, for he coupled Robin Hood not merely with Wat Tyler but with Cade and Kett.) The response to my suggestion was of

the kind which normally comes to young authors only in their
dreams – a letter by return post, saying that the publisher had
been looking for someone to do the job for years, and promising
to commission the story on a synopsis and specimen chapters.
So, almost accidentally, I became a writer for children.

The relevance of these autobiographical fragments will
emerge very soon, as we examine the whole general question
of how the children's author should approach his work.

When preparing this survey I approached several of the most
popular British authors for their views. 'I write for children,'
Enid Blyton told me, 'because: first, I love them and understand
them, and know exactly what they want: secondly, I trained as a
kindergarten Froebel teacher, one of the finest groundings
possible, because of its insistence on the importance of an understanding of children's psychology . . .' Captain Johns wrote
that the work 'demands a peculiar technique based on an understanding of the juvenile mind, which, unless one is born with it,
or retains it from childhood, is not easy to develop.' I am not
clear how one can be born with an understanding of the juvenile
mind – it seems a precocious piece of equipment – but if there is
such a person as 'a born teacher' he too presumably possesses it.
On the whole, though, I think Captain Johns is closer to the
truth when he speaks of retaining it from childhood. I doubt
if it is so much 'an understanding of the juvenile mind' as a
vivid retention of one's own thoughts, feelings and interests,
all those years ago.

People talk of popular authors who know how to 'cater' for
children. They are supposed to study the children around them,
weigh up the rival popularity at the moment of aeroplanes and
submarines, stage-doors and stables, and give the juvenile mind
what it wants. This was the approach recommended to beginners
in such manuals as Arthur Groom's *Writing for Children* and
G. J. H. Northcroft's textbook with the same title. (It is only
fair to say that Groom, till 1963 an active and successful
practitioner, was a very young man when this book came out
in 1929, and that he might have expressed his views quite

differently today.) There is no doubt that much entertainment has been given, and much money made, by authors adopting this advice. But it is questionable how many great children's books have been produced. In other literary fields the policy of giving the public exactly what it wants has always been profitable, but seldom productive of masterpieces. The artist gives what *he* wants. If it is fine, and happens to be what the public wants as well, he is lucky, and achieves success in his lifetime.

Of the world's best-loved children's books many were never intended for the young. Did Swift lean from his Dublin window and play eavesdropper to the urchins below, studying child-psychology so that Gulliver might become a nursery favourite? And Defoe, and the Brothers Grimm, and the outspoken original authors of *The Arabian Nights* – were they deliberately 'catering' for boys and girls?

Turning from these happy accidents, look at some of the classics which were aimed directly at the juvenile mark. *Tom Brown's Schooldays* was written, said its author, 'to get the chance of preaching, and not for any other object'. Tom Brown may not be so popular now as when he was created, nearly a century ago, first in a new field, but he is by no means finished.

In May 1868, an American woman struggling with a story for girls wrote in her diary: 'I plod away, though I don't enjoy this sort of thing. Never liked girls or knew many, except my sisters; but our queer plays and experiences may prove interesting, though I doubt it.' So did the publisher. A month later she recorded that he 'thought it dull; so do I. But work away and mean to try the experiment, for lively, simple books are very much needed for girls, and perhaps I can supply the need.' She did. Louisa Alcott's 'little women' still hold their place in the hearts of many modern girls.

E. Nesbit used to point out how 'by some fortunate magic' she remembered vividly and exactly how she had felt herself as as girl. Virginia Woolf commented somewhere on Lewis Carroll's quality of perpetuating his own childhood, and E. M. Delafield wrote that 'Charlotte Yonge, who lived to be seventy-seven years old, remained emotionally fixed in adolescence'.

Emotional fixation is a high price to pay for popularity as a children's writer, and it would be absurd to suggest that it is always demanded, though it is no doubt commoner than we care to admit – and not only among the dons and old maids but also among some of the retired warriors who turn their hands to red-blooded adventure-stories. But one can have the vivid memory without the emotional fixation, and it is that, I suggest, which has drawn fine sensitive children's books from writers like Walter de la Mare and A. A. Milne, who are no less at home in the adult world.

A writer must of course be conscious of his audience and responsive to it. A children's author will benefit by continually renewing his contact with boys and girls. Even Carroll needed the Dean's daughters to inspire the *Alice* books, but it was rather that they liked what he gave them than that he gave them what they liked. Who in the world (even with Froebel training) could have calculated that *Alice* was the sort of book children would love? There *was* no such 'sort' until Alice appeared. Contact with children is fertilizing. I have seen its influence in my own work – subtle differences between stories written in the masculine atmosphere of a boys' school and tried out, chapter by chapter, on the boarders on wet afternoons, and stories written at home where the daily critic was a schoolgirl. One tries to please, naturally. But when one begins deliberately to 'cater', like a school dietician adding up calories and checking off vitamins, then one begins to write down.

'The fact is I know nothing at all about children!' said the late Arthur Mee. 'What I have always tried to do is to write interestingly and plainly so that anybody would read it. I have never thought of children at all, but just of intelligent people who are eagerly wanting to know and are interested in the great adventure of the world.' Listen also to Anatole France: 'When you are writing for children do not assume a style for the occasion. Think your best and write your best. Let the whole thing live.'

Those were the principles with which I began to write. Experience suggested modifications. We must not really pretend that the child audience and the adult are the same, though some authors, from Defoe to Buchan, have reached both with the one book. There are themes which, if not unsuitable or incomprehensible to the younger reader, at least require different presentation. And there are linguistic problems – not necessarily a smaller vocabulary but an ignorance of secondary meanings and metaphors; the literalness of the child-mind.

When I was little, I was once observed at the back of the house with a plank laid seesaw-fashion across a log, and several heavy volumes piled on either end. Asked what I was doing, I am reminded that I answered solemnly: 'What Daddy does at the office – balancing the books!' But it was not until I went back into the schoolroom early in 1940 and taught English that I saw the wide extent of this literalness. English is a bog full of metaphors and allusions so deeply sunk that the adult is scarcely conscious of a bump beneath his feet, but to the child they may be real obstacles. We write perhaps of 'flogging a dead horse' – and unwittingly perplex our readers with a picture of pointless barbarity, pointlessly introduced into a scene where up to that moment there had been no mention of horses, nor even the faintest hoofbeat in the distance.

The child must learn these things sooner or later, just as he must collect new words. 'I have a natural ability for using simple words and simple language,' says Enid Blyton, 'and for making my stories readable – very essential for children's books.' She voices the common cry of publishers and teachers. Write simply, they beg (or command), you can't write *too* simply. One sympathizes. Until the 1939 war few realized the prevalence of adult illiteracy in Britain. Apart from the numerous 'retarded readers' in our schools, there seems to be an alarmingly low general standard. Experts lament 'a deep-seated unwillingness to have anything to do with print' among school-leavers. For that reason we find some educationists defending trash, because anything seems better than nothing, if it induces a child to read. This should be a challenge to the writer. Good stories *can* be written in simple language. A list of recommended *Books for Retarded Readers* issued by a New Jersey library included

Emil and the Detectives, *Pinocchio* and *Dr. Doolittle*. To stand with these stories is a high enough ambition for most of us. But must every children's book be written in semi-basic? It is obviously a matter of introducing unfamiliar words and phrases carefully, in context which make their meaning plain. And may we not, once in a while, permit ourselves a lovely flourish of sound which the child may enjoy without yet comprehending? There is an instructive story about a little girl who was spending the night away from her parents. At bed-time she announced that she could not possibly go to sleep until she had had the poem about the flying birdies recited to her: it was clearly a beloved and invariable ritual. Host and hostess ransacked their memories, and every anthology in the house, to discover the poem she meant. Guests, patiently waiting for their summons to dinner, were drawn upstairs into conference. Poems were recited involving every kind of bird from Shelley's skylark and Keats' nightingale to Davies' kingfisher and Alice Meynell's robin. The child shook a weary head. Then, with a flash of inspiration a guest asked: 'Were the birdies called echoes?' That was it, she agreed, 'wild echoes flying'. So, soothed with half-comprehended Tennyson, she went blissfully to sleep, and they to dinner.

'The doctrine of "vocabulary limitation",' wrote Frank Whitehead in the National Book League journal, *Books*, in 1959, '(or "word control" as it has sometimes, rather misleadingly, been called) originated in the United States, where its heyday was the period 1925 to 1940. Oddly enough it has reached the peak of its influence in Great Britain just at the time when American educationists have been led increasingly to discard it. To a large extent American disillusionment has been the outcome of practical experience; if you try it for long enough, it will be driven home to you in the end that word-controlled reading matter can't help being awfully dull.' Solemn researchers have spent months in discovering what any parent could have told them in a moment: that children know a lot of words we thought, and sometimes hoped, they did not. At Birmingham in 1955, the *Observer* reported, 'several six-year-olds surprised the researchers with "abracadabra", "bagatelle", "helter-skelter", "helicopter" and "tabernacle". One child even used "quern", meaning a stone handmill. A five-year-old girl who uttered a long sentence at high speed, seeing the woman investigator struggling to write it down, remarked: "That was a difficult one, wasn't it?" '

Every children's story should stand the test of all good prose, that it should be capable of being read aloud. When the reader is a child, sentences need to be fairly short, straightforward, without confusing parentheses and inverted constructions, and complete. By complete I do not mean that one should never permit oneself the omitted verb or the truncated thought suggested by the row of dots. So long as they do not become mannerisms these devices are legitimate means to dramatic effect, but they are also stumbling-blocks to the inexperienced reader aloud.

Grammar and style are the two points most frequently raised by teachers when children's books come under discussion. There is a fairly common idea that many stories are ungrammatical. 'Often so completely ungrammatical' is the actual phrase in a letter before me as I write. Leaving aside comic papers, to be looked at later, I can find almost no foundation for this sweeping charge. True, Arthur Groom, in his *Writing for Children*, emphasized the value of conciseness and told the beginner that it was waste of words to write: 'Mr Something Orother rose from his chair. He was a tall man with fair hair, and was clad in a long dressing-gown that reached almost to the ground.' Instead, he advised, write: 'A tall man, Mr Something Orother's long dressing-gown almost swept the ground as he rose from his chair.' There is little evidence that many young authors adopted this advice. Or, if they did, they must also have followed the counsel given elsewhere in the manual, 'to permit a grammarian to read through what they have written before it is submitted to a publisher.'

'I hope also you will touch the question of style,' an experienced school-librarian wrote to me. 'It is so much worse than it was fifty years ago.' Is it? It is often much less 'literary', which is an excellent thing. There is a great vogue for the story which, whether told in the first or the third person, uses authentic juvenile language throughout. It is not just a question of the 'goshes' and 'wizards' and 'smashings' in the dialogue: the entire narrative is skilfully couched in words and constructions a contemporary child would use. It is a legitimate technique, requiring sympathetic study of children today – for which reason it suffers the disadvantage of dating quickly. It is the juvenile equivalent of a style long fashionable in intellectual circles, the tough story of low life, the tale told by an illiterate. At first the freshness of the method was its own justification. It intensified the reality of the story by enabling the child to identify himself still more closely with the characters. But the continual under-statement and the poverty of vocabulary cloy after a time. Teachers who are fighting a hard battle against the use of 'like' for 'as' ('the ponies are down the field like they usually are when we get home for the hols.') have good cause for complaint when they find popular authors perpetuating the horror even outside the protection of inverted commas. Yes, that *is* how children talk. But until the teaching of English is abandoned as a lost cause, need we sabotage the efforts of the teacher?

Colloquial English we must have. Slang in the dialogue may be unavoidable too – a minimum, at least, to suggest the living speech of children. We pay the price for using it, because the 'smashing' of one brief generation soon follows 'spiffing' and 'corking' into that dustiest museum of all, dead slang, dragging our story with it. I have never forgotten a London teacher who came up to me thirty years ago, and asked me to keep deliberate comical misspellings, mispronunciations, and all such devices out of children's stories. 'We've a hard enough job as it is,' she said, 'trying to turn out children who can spell and talk correctly. Don't make it any harder for us, please.'

Does the young reader care twopence about style? Perhaps not consciously. 'A book,' recalls C. Day Lewis in his auto-biography *The Buried Day*, 'was something I tore through for the story, regardless of the style and impatient of the trimmings.' Theme, action and character will naturally come first. G. J. H.

Northcroft, a former editor of the *Boy's Own Paper*, believed, however, that 'children can feel style just as adults can'. At least, like Jo in *Little Women*, they 'like good strong words that mean something'. How far they are aware and consciously appreciative of the well-chosen epithet, the music of a phrase and the rhythm of a sentence, may be hard to estimate, but when we know how often they will read the same book over and over again we may feel sure that something more than the plot is being absorbed. It would be a happy day when every child could say truthfully, adapting Molière, that he had been reading prose all his life.

CHAPTER THREE

Looking at the Pictures

A CHILD'S first story-books are a field for artistic rather than literary criticism. I am no artist; still less am I an art critic; I can hardly claim even to be free from that instinctive defensive attitude which so many writers adopt when the illustrator comes near their work. One does not forget the frontispiece depicting, with ghoulish realism, the crow-pecked corpse of the hanged outlaw – nor the lost sales which resulted. ('I couldn't put a picture like that in the children's hands,' they said.) One remembers even that drawing of the detective in broad daylight, pipe in mouth, facing the page on which he is described with 'cigarette glowing in the dusk'. It is surprising how often that kind of thing happens in one's early years, until one can demand a sight of the pictures before the blocks are made. Every writer dreams of an inspired illustrator who will read, as well as illustrate, his book. Many such exist. But it is natural that the majority of the really original artists should turn to the books for the younger children, which offer so much more scope – colour, size of page, and ratio of pictures to text – and it is with their work, the true 'picture-books', that our survey had better begin.

'There can't be any harm in this, surely,' says the harassed mother, scrabbling among the books at the cheap chain-stores. 'I mean, it's practically all *pictures* . . .'

Evelyn Gibbs remarks in her *Teaching of Art in Schools* that the child's imagination, when it comes to school, has already been stifled and repressed by, among other things, 'bad picture-books given at an early age'. That great American librarian, Anne Carroll Moore, says in *My Roads to Childhood*: 'There have been many attempts to teach the appreciation of art, but I know of none so effective as giving fine picture-books and drawings right of way with children.' And the Belgian, Jeanne Cappe, writes in her *Contes Bleus, Livres Roses*:

'When I drew the attention of parents to the dangerous complacency which led them to buy their sons these stories, whose poverty of design is reinforced by their ineptitude of text, they answered without reflection, "The youngsters love them!" I am quite sure they also love certain dishes which, in the end, can make them ill. And if you have given them nothing else, how can you expect them to cultivate a taste for anything better?

' "But these pictures amuse them?"

' "Excuse me! These pictures make them snigger . . . It isn't quite the same thing." '

M. McLeish, writing in the *Junior Bookshelf* of March 1944, was of much the same opinion: 'Young children bring their own fresh imaginations to bear upon their gazings; that is why good and bad art are alike to them. Any recognizable symbol will serve to build their vision upon. But it is then that the visual imagination takes root, far below the surface of conscious appreciations. If this be true – and the fact that the average adult reveals a mind, a visual outlook, resembling the weedy débris of a wrecked garden, bears out the statement – then how important that fact is to illustrators of children's books!'

We must keep a sense of proportion. The harm done by bad picture-books must be recognized but not exaggerated. The healthy growing mind is tough in this, as in other respects. It can stand up to a large number of 'pretty' pictures and crude comics without permanent injury. Any scheme for censorship would be utopian, so long as our magazines carry pictorial advertisements and our hoardings posters, and the postman brings hideous cards at Christmas, birthdays and other occasions for family rejoicing. Children will continue to see bad art on all sides, at least in the towns and indoors, for many years to come. But for this very reason it is vitally important to put as much good art as possible into the other scale-pan. Advertisers, though an increasing number in recent years have become art patrons, are under no traditional obligation to be so: their primary business remains the sale of beer or lavender or

whatever it is. Book-publishers, however, have usually acknowledged that they have a cultural as well as a commercial role.
We have therefore a right to expect better taste in our picture-
books than in our posters. We do not always get it. In the last
resort it is the customer – the hasty harassed mother, searching
for something 'to keep the children quiet' – who determines the
standard, for the publisher cannot forget commercial considerations. 'Thus,' says Jeanne Cappe, 'are encouraged the worst
despisers of childhood, those who, in the name of a talent which
they imagine they possess, swamp the market with stupid and
pernicious work. The high price of books has no other reason.
For the size of the edition in the case of the better ones is in-
furiatingly restrained by the superabundance of the mediocre
and worse. "But everything has to be sold!" Yes, and in the
end it is the young readers who suffer for it.'

There is something else to remember. The small child with the
picture-book is forming not merely his taste for art but also his
attitude to books. It is his first encounter with that strange,
infinitely variable article, which can equally well prove a pass-
port to lifelong pleasure or an instrument of punishment or
just a plain bore, useful only as a missile or a door-stop. It is
essential that the child should love his first books. No matter
how great the artist, if his work is not within the comprehension
of the young viewer, if it does not produce genuine pleasure,
it is bad as a child's picture-book. This obvious fact is stressed
only because it is forgotten with such surprising frequency. The
answer to the inartistic book is not the 'arty' one.

'I think,' wrote a member of the Nursery School Association,
'that a more definite explanation of why children like certain
stories at certain ages would not only help the adults in their
choice, but would also add enormously to their own interest
in both the children and their stories.' Agreed. But it is a tall
order, which would be better fulfilled by a competent team of
observers. The classification of books in age-groups is always a
chancey thing. What one child has outgrown at ten, another
is only discovering at twelve. Publishers put rather vague

indications, such as 5–7, in their catalogues. General book-lists are brought out with rough classifications, and so long as children remain individuals we are unlikely to attain anything much more exact.

The very first picture-books, we may agree, should bear a close relationship to the visible world around the child. The earliest aesthetic emotion, through this medium anyhow, seems to be the recognition of the familiar, and this was admirably provided by Kathleen Gell's illustrations to *Come In*, by Olive Dehn. Those of us who are not educationists seldom appreciate

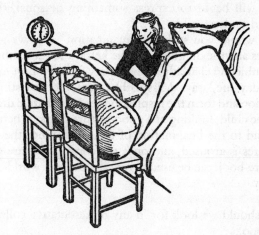

the gulf which is bridged when a child first associates a two-dimensional representation with the solid object it portrays. I never realized it myself until I heard of illiterate sepoys who, coming from villages where hardly a sheet of paper or a photograph existed, could not take in anything two-dimensional until they had adjusted themselves to the convention. It was useless at first to teach them their letters from the blackboard – they could not recognize them again. They had to learn the shapes first by using thick rope, twisted into the required patterns on the grass (this was something they could quite literally 'get hold of'), then by grooves scratched in the sand, and only then with chalk and blackboard. The Western child has never to make this abrupt leap. He surveys the hoardings while still in his perambulator, and his questing fingers soon close, often with disastrous results, round such family photographs as stand within reach. Even so, the natural progression is from chairs to castles, and, as the child realizes that a static drawing can represent life and movement, from dogs to dragons, rather than the reverse. It is the order which a child will normally follow in his own creative drawing. 'The teacher will find,' says Evelyn Gibbs, 'that it is by making pictures of incidents connected with their everyday lives, within their own experience, that the children will begin to express something personal, that they know and understand.'

What, would you stifle the imagination? No, we go on to the castles and the dragons, but the kettle and the clothes-horse and the rubicund charlady are necessary first. 'Robust memories of everyday life,' says Miss Gibbs, 'are the real stimulus to imagination and form the inspiration for imaginative drawings.' So too the child, looking at a good picture-book, is better fitted to respond to the imagination of the artist. Once the appetite for pictures is aroused, and once the conventions are grasped, the picture-book can be used to reveal the whole world of reality and fancy.

What should we look for in any representative collection of picture-books?

Other things being equal, that it should contain pictures in a wide range of styles and media, the best available of each kind. The youngest child may be attracted first to the gayest colour. Let's have it, primitive, crude if you like. It is impossible to define in words just where crudity becomes vulgarity – it is all bound up with spontaneity and sophistication, and the individual book-buyer will probably judge in a highly subjective way. When there are still more good picture-books in the shops, and fewer bad ones, we shall be less at the mercy of our own ill-trained taste. On the whole, clean colours matter more than just bright ones. Few can have given as much joy to children as the pastel shades of the Beatrix Potter pictures.

One would like every child to have free range along shelves carrying a little of everything, from the classic to the contemporary. And a very considerable range it could be. The selection of even first alphabet books runs from Kate Greenaway's old-world *A – Apple Pie* (of which Ruskin, however, declared that the lettering was 'bill-sticking of the vulgarest sort' and the drawings possessed not 'the least melodious charm') through *Babar's ABC* by Jean de Brunhoff, Roger Duvoisin's *A for the Ark*, and other notable variations on the theme to *Brian Wildsmith's A.B.C.*, appropriately awarded the Library Association's Kate Greenaway Medal as the outstanding picture-book of 1962.

Only by putting real variety within the child's reach can we discover whether he, as an individual, truly shares any of his elders' nostalgic enthusiasm for Tenniel, Randolph Caldecott, Arthur Rackham, Charles Folkard, Ernest H. Shepard, and the other famous illustrators of the past. He may like some or all of these (it is simplest and least expensive to experiment by leaving around such volumes as survive from our own childhood), but it will be surprising – and should be disturbing – if he does not more often prefer the work of later hands, including some that affronts and exasperates the adult looking over his shoulder. He may delight in the horrific drawings of Mervyn Peake (which I confess I do not) whose *Captain Slaughterboard Drops Anchor*, says Frank Eyre in his monograph, *20th Century Children's Books*, 'has become a focus of argument for those who strongly resent the encroachment of contemporary illustrative techniques into children's books. Printed on blue, pink and yellow paper with grotesque and even macabre-looking figures scattered in seeming incoherence about its pages, it has the most unusual appearance of any modern British picture-book' (that is, up to 1952) 'and it is not altogether surprising that so many people should be startled by it. But children are commonly a good deal tougher than parents appear to imagine . . .' However, even that catholic critic, Kathleen Lines, says cautiously, in *Four to Fourteen*, that this 'realistically imaginative tale of bold bad pirates' is 'not a book to give indiscriminately to any child', and I am inclined to agree. Though it goes against the grain for any writer to admit the greater potency of the picture rather than the written word, I think that in the realm of the horrific it is possible for some illustrations to do harm to some children in a sense that the most vivid phrasing cannot. This applies to very few books, old or new. If Mervyn Peake seems unsuitable for a particular child, there is no lack of other talented modern artists to fill the gap.

The new school of illustrators do not differ from the old merely because they were born fifty or a hundred years later. Frank Eyre, as a publisher, writes expertly in his monograph on the way in which the British picture-book was gradually and belatedly revolutionized, from the nineteen-thirties onwards, partly by French and American influences (the latter in themselves cosmopolitan) and partly by technical changes such as the use of colour lithography instead of the traditional colour half-tone. Today the standard of the British picture-book is high.

Edward Ardizzone's *Tim* stories, Kathleen Hale's *Orlando* books, Joan Kiddell-Monroe's early panda story, *In His Little Black Waistcoat* (forerunner of so much inspired illustration of of the old legends and folk-tales), Rex Whistler's *Hans Andersen* – these and many more are surely worthy to stand beside the best of Grandmother's childhood favourites and beside such contemporary foreign 'guest-artists' as the *Babar* books of Jean de Brunhoff and his nephew Laurent, the *Père Castor* series illustrated by the Lithuanian, Feodor Rojankovsky, and the *Anatole* stories by Eve Titus and Paul Galdone. Nor can I forbear to mention here, since they are truly picture-books – big, flat and gloriously colourful – though their text is not for the smaller child, Clarke Hutton's *Picture Histories* of Britain, France, Italy, and other countries, J. B. Priestley's *Story of the Theatre* (illustrated by a whole team of artists), and the Giant Golden Books, notably the one of *Bible Stories from the Old Testament* (Rojankovsky again the illustrator) and the companion *Stories from the New Testament*, in which the pictures are the work of Alice and Martin Provensen.

What about colour-photography? We have had books in which obvious dolls and stuffed animals have been photographed in tableaux to illustrate nursery classics like *Aladdin, Cinderella*, and *The Seven Ravens*. I have already shuddered at a sawdust *Wind in the Willows*. No one knows on what target the sacrilegious lens will next be turned. The effect of the camera on really imaginative writing is as lethal as that of a machine-gun. How many of us would choose to read, say, *Wuthering Heights* in an edition garnished with stills from the film? Why then should we offer children the coloured photograph of a stuffed toy Toad? Colour-photography has a legitimate but limited place in the bookshelf. It is all right for a completely matter-of-fact story like Elsie M. Harris's *Christmas at Timothy's*, where Gee Denes used it to show real people getting out of real trains and sitting round real Christmas dinners. Here the camera is used as it should be, to reveal and heighten the beauty in ordinary everyday scenes. But when the illustrators approach the frontiers of Fairyland, all cameras should be confiscated.

The value of a good picture-book is not solely visual. Even the shortest text, in the kind which carries only a line or two per page, can be well written. The words will be repeated often, until the child announces them at the turning of the page, without being able or needing to spell out the letters. As Margery Fisher says in *Intent Upon Reading*, 'A child's taste in words, no less than in the visual arts, gets its start here, for better or for worse'. So they had better be good, however simple. There is the simplicity of Bunyan as well as the simplicity of *Beano*, though I am all for the gaiety of the latter if it can be achieved without the accompanying vocabulary. Beatrix Potter is the classic example of a good text wedded to good illustrations. Many have already remarked how she did not sacrifice everything to a monotonous, monosyllabic easiness, but occasionally put in a linguistic high-light (for example her celebrated use of the word 'soporific') which merely intensified the pleasure of the young listener.

The themes and content of picture-books are not without

importance. It is possible to say quite enough in a few hundred words and, by the right pictures, to hammer home the impression until it is unforgettable. There is, for instance, Helen A. Monsell's *Paddy's Christmas*, in which Kurt Wiese depicts a 'brown bouncing bear cub named Paddy', turning somersaults down snowy mountain-sides, bothering the grown-up bears who only want to hibernate in peace, and finally introducing them to the human institution of Christmas. The moral of this story is one which needs tactful stressing in many homes at that season: in effect, that Christmas means something more than the receipt of presents and the putting up of decorations. No child would notice the moral, but it might sink in.

As a means of introducing a young child to the life of other nations, the picture-book can be invaluable. A committee of the American Library Association has pointed out that 'really good foreign picture-books are the happiest possible introduction to international feeling', and it is obvious that pictures transplant better than a text which needs translation.

The whole field of picture-books (not to mention pictures in books for the older child) is so vast that only a separate survey could do anything like justice to it. For technical reasons good picture-books were late off the mark. We may date them perhaps

from Kate Greenaway's *Under the Window*, which first established her position in 1878, and was followed by the work of her French counterpart, Boutet de Monvel, whose *Nos Enfants, Filles et Garçons, Jeanne d'Arc*, and other books were published between 1883 and 1897. In the intervening years the picture-book has enlisted in its service many of the most original artists in Europe and America, and the only surprising thing is that so much poor work is still accepted.

CHAPTER FOUR

Fancy Free

FAIRY-Tales – if the word is used in its common, loose sense to cover legend, folk-literature, and modern fantasy – are the only children's books about which adults argue very much in the ordinary way. They are the happy hunting-ground of anthropologists, philologists, psychologists, and other learned men. It is intellectually respectable to write them – was not Carroll a mathematician and have not Professors J. B. S. Haldane, J. R. R. Tolkien, and C. S. Lewis made notable contributions in our own time? Frank Eyre says that 'the majority of genuine writers when writing for children turn instinctively to fantasy, leaving the story of everyday life, with rare exceptions, to the second-raters', and though the 'rare exceptions' have included such 'genuine writers' as Mark Twain, John Masefield, Richard Church, C. Day Lewis, Lawrence Durrell, Enid Bagnold, and P. H. Newby, his statement is generally valid. So, too, if an adult reader returns for any reason to children's books, he is more easily attracted to the fantastic. Realism he can find more deeply and (for his mature mind) more satisfyingly treated in adult literature. In fantasy, on the other hand, he finds a pleasure afforded only by the children's book. This natural bias too often unbalances such serious criticism of juvenile literature as we yet possess, weighting the scales in favour of what is 'amusing', 'charming', and 'delightful' and against what is merely 'exciting' and 'dramatic'. For the child both types of story have equal value, since each meets a distinct need. We should, incidentally, differentiate between the two meanings of 'fantasy', for in the other sense of day-dreaming, a sense made popular by the psychologists, it also enters into numerous books which, while superficially 'realistic', are in plot and situation absurdly and misleadingly unreal.

40

Fairies in the strict sense hardly ever appear in books written nowadays. They are perhaps self-conscious since *Iolanthe* and *Peter Pan*. They have had a long run for their money – they are a genuine British product in the ancient sense, for their life runs back past Herrick and Shakespeare and Drayton, past Chaucer's Wife of Bath, to the ancient Celts, before Roman Civil Servants came out on the heels of Agricola and began the first hopeless attempt to instil reason into the islanders.

Even the fairies have found the twentieth century rather a strain. 'The steam-engine routs Faërie,' says Walter de la Mare. He goes on, tracing the development of the modern child: 'Actuality breaks in upon dream. School rounds off the glistening angles. The individual is swamped awhile by the collective. Yet the child mind, the child imagination, persists, and, if powerful, never perishes.' I take this to mean that if the child is tough enough, he can survive even the raising of the school-leaving age.

It is not so much the steam-engine that is routing Faërie, so far as the publishers' lists are concerned. It is the Disneyfied banality of the cheap fairy-book as sold in chain-stores and small stationers'. Here is the recipe for commercial success given in Groom's manual: 'Plenty of dialogue and dainty descriptive writing is essential in tales of this kind, but the author must be wary of introducing too much "sob-stuff" . . . The "sob-stuff" must be daintily administered in small doses . . . The dragon story is in a class by itself. Some writers specialize in such tales, frequently with considerable success, but the really successful writer combines dragons with giants and dwarfs.' That 'sob-stuff daintily administered in small doses' was the poison which has decimated fairies in contemporary fiction. Anyone following such advice deserves to be pixy-led and transformed into something more harmless than a writer of bad books for children. And may the only royalties he ever sees be Oberon and Titania, terrible of brow, as he quakes and grovels before their thrones.

If our children are to have fairies, let them be fairies worthy of their magic powers and lineage, so that the children may sing in the words of *The Immortal Hour*:

> How beautiful they are, the Lordly Ones,
> That dwell in the hollow hills!
> They have faces like flowers—

That is how fairies should look, not like the chubby, frilly girlies from the local dancing-class, with pink paper wings drooping from the safety-pins between their shoulder-blades. Let them be friends on whom the child can count, but let it also be remembered that they can be potent enemies if unjustly used. There should be an element of pleasurable terror in the thought of them, comparable with that delicious shudder which runs down the spine as the harp-strings twang in Rutland Boughton's music, or as the stage darkens on a good production of the *Dream* and Puck is

> sent with broom before,
> To sweep the dust behind the door.

It is pleasant to think that Robin Hood must have believed in fairies, that the future London business man, Richard Whittington, must have enjoyed Robin Hood stories in boyhood as much as we do, and that by about 1600 young Herrick was enjoying tales not only of fairies and Robin Hood but of Dick Whittington and his cat. For centuries the literature of Fancy rolled through England like a beneficent snowball, picking up cold history in fragments and rolling it into a new shape. Is it true that *Little Jack Horner* began as a scurrilous rhyme against those who profited from the dissolution of the monasteries, and that *Mary, Mary, Quite Contrary* was the Tudor Queen, viewed through disapproving Protestant eyes, 'the little maids all in a row' being her Catholic nuns? A fine hare to start ... We must not follow it. We must stick to 'tales', leaving aside verse and drama.

Two and a half centuries ago the native stocks of Fancy began to be increased by foreign importation. Cinderella landed, with the rest of Perrault's collection, about 1700. The first English version of *The Arabian Nights* arrived in 1704. Grimm's fairy-tales, originally the by-product of philological research, were translated between 1823 and 1826. Hans Andersen followed in 1846, and then a great flood of stories from France, Germany, Scandinavia and other countries. The sixties were a vintage period in England – *The Water Babies, Alice* and Jean Ingelow's *Mopsa the Fairy* marked the beginning of the third phase. Having gathered up first the folk-lore of Britain and then that of Europe and Asia, the snowball was after original modern work.

Parallel with this development rolled the smaller snowball of the animal story. There had been Dorothy Kilner's *Perambulations of a Mouse* long before. In 1802 there had been *Marvellous Adventures or The Vicissitudes of A Cat* and *Little Juba: The Adventures of a Lap Dog*, and in 1819 *The Rambles of a Butterfly*. In view of the titles it is hardly surprising that the animal story (as distinct from books which introduced animals like the White Rabbit as secondary characters) did not arrive at full popularity until the turn of the century, with Kipling's *Jungle Books* in 1894–5 and Kenneth Grahame's *Wind in the Willows* in 1908. We should distinguish between the type of story in which mice ride motor-cycles and those in which animals are depicted realistically. The second type is fanciful only in so far as the human writer must resort to guess-work when he suggests the thoughts and feelings of animals, and he might maintain that there is only a difference of degree between this and, say, the 'realistic' historical novel. Can we be any surer we know the monk's brain than the monkey's? Mercifully, in this book we are not called upon to catalogue precisely. This merely seems a convenient point to mention both types of story, and to add that there is a certain amount of friction between them. Some of the naturalist writers object strongly to the humanized creatures. If they had their way no Toads should have driving licences. One author protested in a literary paper that such stories falsified Nature, gave children the wrong attitude to animals and could even lead to positive cruelty. She instanced a small boy who had tormented his pet by trying to dress it up like the animals shown in his books. One doubts if such extreme results are common. It is not often one finds a dormouse in the tea-pot.

Condemnation of another kind came from a conference of rabbit clearance societies, when a speaker declared: 'The rabbit has been glorified in the past. Beatrix Potter books in the nursery have meant young people growing up to think of rabbits as little darlings. We should think of doing something to put into the minds of both town and country children the idea that the rabbit is a pest.'

As a pendant let us quote once more from our invaluable handbook: 'With stories dealing with Dame Nature the writer must be sure of the facts before writing a line . . . Every would-be writer should visit a Zoo or Botanic Garden at least once every two years, if that is at all possible.' There are quite a number of animal stories about, which read as though their authors had done just that.

The conflict over animals is little more than a tiff compared with the deeper controversies which have racked Fairyland for more than a century. Moralists have always regarded that region with distrust. There are clear implications in *Midsummer Night's Dream* that Oberon's private life was somewhat irregular, but open criticism was hampered by his being Shakespearean and royal. A character with this double handicap could scarcely hope to go straight. Criticism focused on other sins more suited to the juvenile understanding.

Oliver Goldsmith wanted Dick Whittington rewritten as a moral example to industrious apprentices. The cat, being normally non-productive (at least in the economic sense), would have been liquidated entirely. Samuel Goodrich of New England, the original 'Peter Parley', attacked the 'stories of Little Red Riding Hood, Puss in Boots, Bluebeard, Jack the Giant-killer, and some other of the tales of horror, commonly put into the hands of youths, as if for the express purpose of reconciling them to vice and crime. Some children, no doubt, have a ready appetite for these monstrosities, but to others they are revolting, until by repetition and familiarity the taste is sufficiently degraded to relish them.' We have already seen what another moralist thought of Cinderella.

It was no one-sided battle. As early as 1802 Godwin proclaimed that in children's books imagination was more important than knowledge. Sir Richard Phillips produced his *Popular Fairy Tales* in 1818, just before the Grimms appeared, and another knight, Sir Henry Cole, rode into the lists against 'Peter Parley' in the eighteen-forties, when the battle reached its height. From that date the moralists began to execute a long retreat, with little more than a splutter of a rearguard action when Carlyle denounced *The Arabian Nights* as 'downright lies' and refused to have such 'unwholesome literature' in the house.

The moralists attacked from another flank after the First World War. In Russia the fairies were liquidated as efficiently as the *kulaks*. Later they were brought back – fairies are fortunately immortal – and became as permissible in children's books as they are in opera and ballet. But in the early years of the Revolution it was different. 'Every fantastic and religious element is carefully excluded and replaced by a healthy, bold realism calculated to stimulate children to action and the study of realities.' As an example of this tendency the books published in 1930 included *Ot Kauchuka do Galoshy*, 'the different stages through which rubber passes before it becomes a galosh', a picture-book designed for the delectation of the under-sevens.

About the same period, Berwick Sayers tells us in his manual on children's libraries, fairy-tales were banished from many American schools. 'Fairies do not exist; they mislead the child's imagination; therefore, in some way they are inimical; they must be banished from nursery and school. . . . The very notion,' he comments, 'is an adult impertinence.' Meanwhile in China the Governor of Honan Province was banning *Alice*: 'Bears, lions and other beasts cannot use a human language, and to attribute to them such power is an insult to the human race. Any child reading such books must inevitably regard animals and human beings on the same level, and this would be disastrous.' Grimm was banned in the British Zone of Germany in 1947. It was argued that in the special circumstances, i.e. the necessity for deliberate mass re-education of a Hitler-hypnotized nation, this drastic surgical treatment was unavoidable.

Many people have had their doubts about Grimm's tales, which were not, after all, collected originally for children. An element of the horrific is all right up to a point. 'Stories such as "Blue-Beard" and "Jack the Giant-killer",' Bertrand Russell has maintained, 'do not involve any knowledge of cruelty whatever. To the child they are purely fantastic, and he never connects them with the real world in any way.' Alison Uttley recalls from her own childhood 'this mixture of fear and delight'. 'We were afraid, but we loved the tales,' she says. 'I was certain the beasts were lying awake in the darkness . . . Perhaps they were on the stairs . . .' But it is not Grimm she is remembering. There will always be differences of opinion about horrific stories and pictures, if only because what arouses one parent with screams from the next bedroom in the middle of the night will leave the offspring of another quite unaffected. Harvey Darton, in his history of children's books, declares roundly that the adult disapproval of fairy-tales 'is a manifestation, in England, of a deep-rooted sin-complex. It involves the belief that anything fantastic on the one hand, or anything primitive on the other, is inherently noxious, or at least so void of good as to be actively dangerous.' And Jeanne Cappe says: 'Let us leave the children to penetrate fearlessly into the kingdom of fiction; let us leave them to associate with enchanters and good fairies in dawn-hued robes, nimble gnomes, industrious goblins. They will only be better for it. They will only be fitter to become men.'

Will they? Entertainment apart, what virtue is there in the fairy-tale? Remember our tentative definition of a good children's book in the opening chapter. 'To stimulate the imagination . . . or to educate the emotions.' A good fairy-tale can certainly do the former, and perhaps also the latter. Paul Hazard would have said so. 'A Perrault,' he wrote, 'while he is relating marvels to us, teaches us with wit and charm not to be mistaken about men, women and children; he is full of observation and he is never ponderous. He has so many delightful traits, so just and so true, that they penetrate the soul deeply;

so full of strength that they will ripen gradually in the spirit to blossom some day into wisdom.' There is no doubt that the fairy-tale – not Perrault's only, not the primitive story only, but the modern one as well – is a good medium for the interpretation of human nature. Listen to this dialogue in Mary Norton's *Bonfires and Broomsticks*:

'But,' stammered Emelius, '. . . the love philtre—'
'Coloured water,' said the old necromancer in a tired voice.
'And foretelling the future?'
'Nothing in it . . . Whatever you prophesy about the future comes true if you don't go into details, and what doesn't come true they forget.'

This book, now incorporated with its predecessor in a single volume, *Bed Knob and Broomstick*, is one of the best examples of modernized magic. A bedstead takes the place of the traditional flying carpet, voyaging through space in the first book and time in the second. There is a witch one can believe in, a genteel village lady who would be a pillar of any Women's Institute, but who in strict privacy is learning magic by correspondence. Her powers are thus strictly limited, which is an excellent idea, because omnipotence is very dull. The humour, though it delighted this particular adult, is not of the sly sophisticated kind which aims at the parent over the child's head. We *do* get that kind nowadays: I read, in a book which in general style was clearly intended for young children, a dig at 'George Bernard Owl, the wisest and most celebrated of all the Owl philosophers; the only owl who did not eat mice, but lived off nuts like the squirrels and had a plan for everybody'. *Bed Knob and Broomstick* makes no such mistake. It is a worthy addition to that large group of books in which modern children are transported to the Past – E. Nesbit's *The Story of the Amulet*, Kipling's *Puck of Pook's Hill* and *Rewards and Fairies*, Alison Uttley's *Traveller in Time* (one of the most original, because the transfer is of a psychic character), Patricia Lynch's *The Turf-cutter's Donkey* and Hilda Lewis's *Ship that Flew*. Mary Norton's stories, originally published in 1945 and 1947, were the first fruits of a rich crop of fresh 'Time' fantasies which appeared in the nineteen-fifties – Philippa Pearce's *Tom's Midnight Garden*, Edward Eager's *The Time Garden*, M. Pardoe's *Argle* stories, David Severn's *Drum-beats!* and *The Future Took Us*, Ronald Welch's *The Gauntlet*, Noel Streatfeild's *The Fearless Treasure*, Meriol Trevor's *Sun Slower, Sun Faster*, and Nan Chauncy's Tasmanian *Tangara* by no means exhaust the list but are enough to demonstrate the infinitely varied twists which can be given to this idea by different writers. Miss Norton meantime had turned her talents in another direction and created a race of fascinating miniature creatures, whose adventures she narrated in *The Borrowers* and subsequent volumes. We have heard no more, alas, of that splendid modern witch, but the nineteen-fifties produced two other spell-binding ladies with certain literary affinities, though each the distinctively original creation of her respective author – Dowsabel in Lorna Wood's *Hag* stories, and the ex-owner of the cat Carbonel in Barbara Sleigh's story of that name and its sequel, *The Kingdom of Carbonel*.

The traditional fairy-tale has far more aesthetic possibilities than most types of story. Writer and illustrator have a free hand. Enchanted woodlands, turrets on crystal crags, breathlessly beautiful princesses, magic sailing-ships, soft-eyed reindeer and blue-shadowed snow are less limiting than tousled schoolgirls nattering in the dorm or goggled motorists racing round Silverstone. Beauty is the essence of the fairy-tale. Real ugliness has no place there – the grotesqueness of gnomes and gnarled but kindly woodcutters, and of crazy cottages which even the most backward rural authority would condemn, enters the fairy-tale only for the sake of contrast, so that the beauty of goose-girl and palace may be enhanced.

Many fairy-tales have made good ballets. Conversely, in judging a fairy-tale – or in writing one, in so far as it is still possible to write new ones – something like the symmetry of the ballet should be sought. Observe the repetitive pattern which is so characteristic a feature of the folk-tale, and observe how the small child, hearing such a story read aloud, appreciates the repetitions and delights in the expected climax. Three wishes, seven sons – the numbers three and seven are always recurring. The wandering hero meets a succession of people on his quest. To each he puts the same question in the same words (he does not, like a real-life salesman or social investigator, change his approach to suit the income-group of the interviewed), but it is the strangers who answer in varied terms. Not for them the monotonous 'couldn't say, I'm sure' of the real world. While admitting personal ignorance they refer him, with the deftness of an information bureau, to 'my brother, the West Wind' or 'the old bear who lives in the glass cave beyond the golden mountain'. It is such variations which, imposed upon a basic pattern, combining the expected and the unexpected in just the right proportions, give the child aesthetic satisfaction comparable with that which adults derive from good choreography or symphonic composition. And aesthetic education at the same time.

So, too, with style and vocabulary. There is no excuse here for verbal poverty. The narrator is not trying to pretend he is a tight-lipped bomber-pilot or a healthily illiterate hippomaniac. Pile on the colour, exaggerate the effects, cut out the 'somewhats' and the 'rathers' – this is not *The Times Literary Supplement*. Not that the effects must be strained. Spontaneity is all. Fancy is free to use the academic polysyllables of Lewis Carroll, the polished prose of Ruskin and Wilde or the racy, poetic homeliness of the folk-tale.

Boris Artzybasheff's *Seven Simeons* is a superb example of that. The pictures are a joy in themselves – they have all the intricacy and formality of Byzantine art, curling across the large pages in red and green and gold, conventional yet somehow intensely alive. There is verbal artistry in such sentences as: 'His thoughts were like entangled black threads. He could never find the end to them;' and: 'in less time than it takes to braid the hair on a bald man's head'. In the ending too:

The church bells pealed, the flags waved and the cannons fired the salutes until they burst.

It was a fine party! I should know because I was there myself and danced to the gay music till I couldn't dance any more.

And now, my gentle friends, we are at the tale's end. For what was good in it, praise it; but for the rest forgive the poor story-teller. A wrong word is not like the bird in a cage. If ever a word flies out, no man can jump and catch it. In this I have no doubt.

It is that combination of homely poetry and humour which makes the Irish so pre-eminent in the literature of fancy. Whether it is James Stephens or Padraic Colum, poets in their own right, re-telling ancient folk-tales or blind Frances Browne dictating *Granny's Wonderful Chair*, or Patricia Lynch creating original stories like *The Turf-cutter's Donkey*, that amazingly persistent, pervading national excellence is there. Dorothy Neal White seems to underline that point about aesthetic education when she says that 'an Irish fairy-tale read at ten may well be preparation for Yeats's *Tower* read at thirty'.

Children should have access to the best possible collection of fairy-tales, told and illustrated in the best way, from every country with stories to contribute. The Oxford University Press has produced, over the past decade, its beautiful *Myths and Legends* series, working its way round the world from *English Fables and Fairy Stories* to *Japanese Tales and Legends*. Joan Kiddell-Monroe's gracefully sweeping, always unmistakable illustrations, in both colour and black-and-white, are the constant element in a collection which is inevitably uneven in interest, because of the varying worth of the material and the text, contributed by diverse writers not all as good story-tellers as they are scholars. For a family bookshelf, with strict limitations of space and spending power, it may be better to resist the temptation to collect the set (splendid though they look in full array) and to choose a few volumes of special appeal, mingled with other, individual books – perhaps Amabel Williams-Ellis's *Fairy Tales from the British Isles*, Zoë Zajdler's *Polish Fairy Tales*, or H. Herda's comprehensive *Fairy Tales from Many Lands*. For Grimm, Andersen, and *The Arabian Nights* there are four or five good editions each offered by various publishers, and it is well worth waiting to compare them, in a well-stocked children's book department, before committing oneself.

So it was with Robin Hood and King Arthur and the Greek legends. Robin has engaged the attention of at least three of our leading writers since this survey first appeared – Carola Oman (*Robin Hood, the Prince of Outlaws*), Rosemary Sutcliff (*The Chronicle of Robin Hood*), and Roger Lancelyn Green (*Robin Hood*), while Mr Green's *King Arthur and the Knights of the Round Table* and *Heroes of Greece and Troy* share the honours in these fields with Barbara Leonie Picard's *Stories of King Arthur and His Knights, The Iliad,* and *The Odyssey.* From the same pens come also, respectively, *Myths of the Norsemen* and *Tales of the Norse Gods and Heroes.* All these themes have been treated by various other writers as well, notably the *Iliad* in Robert Graves' *The Siege and Fall of Troy.* It is difficult to find territory untrodden within the past few years (though E. M. Almedingen achieved it notably in *The Knights of the Golden Table*, with Vladimir of Kiev as a welcome change from Arthur of Camelot), for when Miss Sutcliff rewrites *Beowulf* she is not long behind Ian Serraillier's poetic *Beowulf the Warrior*, and her admirable *Hound of Ulster: The story of Cuchulain* was preceded by *Cuchulain, The Hound of Ulster* by Eleanor Hull.

There is wide agreement that over-production, in the sense of unnecessary multiplication of titles, is the bane of children's literature. Too many different books are published, selling on average too few copies, with a consequent production cost which is reflected in the price. Sixpence a copy on the printing bill may mean another one-and-sixpence by the time the book is handed across the counter. It would hardly be fair, though, to regard the various versions of the classics as an example of this deplorable duplication – provided, at least, that no new edition is offered to the public without some distinctive merit of its own. Publishers cannot be expected to grant any single rival a monopoly in one of the sure-selling immortals. Illustrators cannot be denied the freedom to interpret the age-old stories in their own way. It is good that people who prefer the draughtsmanship of an earlier generation should still be able to find it – and good, too, that others should have choice among the contemporary artists. No one admires more than I do the fecund talent of Joan Kiddell-Monroe, but I would no more wish children to see the whole world of folk-tale and legend through her eyes exclusively than I would wish her artificially to restrict her output. So with the writers. So long as distinguished authors like those named above find satisfaction in re-telling the traditional stories, they are surely entitled to please themselves. It would be time enough to lament if there were any sign that, for example, Miss Sutcliff was being distracted from her primary work as an imaginative fiction-writer.

Let us suppose, then, that we have made our personal selection and filled half the bookshelf with the sort of stuff which should be the heritage of every child, to accept or to reject, but always to be offered. What shall we put in the other half? Carroll and Kipling and Kenneth Grahame, Masefield and Milne and de la Mare? The selection is wide, the decision must be individual. But in addition to all the authors and titles already mentioned I would respectfully submit this short list of candidates for consideration: *Birl: The Story of a Cat* by the Swiss Alexander M. Frey; something of Eleanor Farjeon's rich output, perhaps her own version of Cinderella, *The Glass Slipper*, or *The Perfect Zoo*, with its repartee worthy of Humpty Dumpty himself and magnificent coloured pictures by Kathleen Burrell; Nicholas Stuart Gray's *Over the Hills to Fabylon*; Joan Aiken's brilliantly funny *All You've Ever Wanted*; and *A Bear Called Paddington* by Michael Bond.

No child with such a shelf will suffer from imaginative mal-nutrition. There will be no need for 'sob-stuff', even in small doses.

CHAPTER FIVE

The Fringe of Fact

PROSE fiction is our present topic, but not all that is classed in libraries as 'non-fiction' lies outside our terms of reference. True, we are turning our backs resolutely on poems and plays, on all the 'how-to-do-its', 'how-to-make-its' and 'how-to-collect-thems', on encyclopaedias, outlines, symposia on careers, the wonders of science and so forth. But there remain several shelves of highly debatable territory.

Many years ago I wrote a book with an Indian setting. It introduced many real characters – William Hawkins, the Emperor Jehangir, and others – and it was concerned with a real journey, the first mission of the East India Company to the mainland.

Ten years later I wrote another book with a modern Indian setting. It contained no real persons and was concerned with the imaginary journey of a boy and girl through India and Pakistan.

The first book is always quite properly shelved as a juvenile historical novel, and the second as non-fiction. The arrangement sounds illogical, but it works, and corresponds to the essential nature and purpose of the respective books. The example may serve to show how impossible it is to draw precise boundaries.

The didactic story fills the modern adult with horror. It is, if possible, even worse than a story with a moral. Anthony Delius' *The Young Traveller in South Africa* was thus reviewed in *The School Librarian*, more in sorrow than in anger: 'As soon as Father decides to take young Dick with him on his business trip to South Africa (by air, of course), the book fails. No boy (except Dick) could believe in such a father. No boy (except Dick) could believe in such a boy. He asks all the appropriate questions and gets all the appropriate answers. Now and again his true boyishness is allowed to assert itself: he revolts from lectures on history and retires to eat ice-cream. The lectures are disguised as casual conversation; but even young Dick can see through the disguise. This, I feel sure, is not the way to write for the young. The theory is that the average boy will identify himself with young Dick and have a thoroughly pleasant and informative tour of South Africa . . . The fact is that the average boy will call the whole thing a "swizz".'

Now that is a good honest, hard-hitting review of which no author would complain. But, the book's literary imperfections admitted, is it fair to judge it by the standards applicable to pure fiction? It is quite obvious, on opening it, that here is a great deal of information to be conveyed to anyone interested. There are excellent photographs, a map, an index and a pronouncing glossary. 'The average boy' sees at once what he is in for – these are not the normal equipment of an adventure-story. If he reads the book it will be, presumably, because he wants to hear about South Africa. In which case he will find it anything but a 'swizz'. Time has, indeed, so little endorsed the reviewer's judgement that the book has gone into successive new impressions, and it has been the first of a long series, by different writers in the same manner, which has achieved world-wide popularity in various languages. Many countries are also covered in the 'We Go' series – *We Go to Germany*, and so on.

I am not so sure that the didactic story worries the child as much as the adult. Has there ever been a more blatant example than *The Swiss Family Robinson*? Even the critical modern child is prepared to swallow pages of instruction on boat-building, the care of ponies, and the L.C.C. regulations on the employment of juvenile actors – and this even in what ranks as pure fiction. We may not go all the way with J. G. Wilson, the librarian, writing in *The Family Book* that 'the primary demand of children is not for amusement, but for facts. Most children can amuse themselves if they are left to their own resources; but they cannot get at the facts about the world in which they find themselves without help.' But the appetite for facts is certainly strong.

Of course, retort the critics, but it all depends on how they are presented. You could never accuse Arthur Ransome and the others of being didactic. . . . True, so long as one does not try to give *much* information, one escapes the charge. Suppose, though, there is a great deal of information to be given?

It is possible to give a lively picture of one aspect of a country in pure fiction: that is worth doing and will be deservedly popular. It is possible to give a balanced, factual account of that same country, in all its aspects, with no dialogue and no fictitious characters: that is hardly worth doing, because few children want what is indistinguishable from a textbook. The first book is too limited and the second is useless. We can either hand over to the travel-film, or do what we can with the didactic story. It may be a mongrel art form, but mongrels are sometimes conspicuous for their brightness and intelligence.

To the writer such books present technical problems which are fascinating and maddening by turns. He is trying at once to cover the ground and to tell a story. He must steer between the Scylla of *The School Librarian* (and many a less sympathetic reviewer) and the Charybdis of the expert only too ready to cry: 'What? A book on South Africa which does not mention the Asiatic minority problem?'

The author must strive continually to make his facts emerge naturally and unobtrusively from his fiction, but he cannot hope to manage it all the time unless he is allowed ten times the space. He must sometimes be permitted characters who 'ask all the appropriate questions and get all the appropriate answers'. It was a technique used quite effectively by the older writers, including one named Plato.

The trouble with travel stories is that, the more important the country covered, the more often they require rewriting. Marjorie Fischer's *Palaces on Monday*, for example, gave a useful picture of the Soviet Union in the glowing light of the middle nineteen-thirties, but is now as much out of date as Ilin's *Moscow Has A Plan*. Both are such excellent books in their entirely different ways that they are still worth a place on the shelf, but the

E

Russias they depict are already receding into history, and books like Wright Miller's *Young Traveller in Russia* (or, for younger children, Noel Streatfeild's *Lisa Goes to Russia* and Joan Charnock's *Russian Twins*) are needed to correct false impressions. The same is true of all the principal countries; not that the smallest stand still, but it is hardly an economic proposition to bring out a new book on Norway every five years. The publishers of *The Young Traveller* books make a very conscientious effort to keep their volumes up to date.

The situation is quite different when we turn to the exploration and revelation of our own countryside. Much remains to be done here, but some good books – notably the 'Romany' series – are available. Malcolm Saville, an author with an intense feeling for the English scene, and a determination to share it with his readers, uses a wide variety of authentic regional backgrounds, and his stories have led many boys and girls to the actual scenes described. But the essential Saville, I think he would himself agree, is contained in the book, *Jane's Country Year*, where the story is subordinated to the country lore. Here is didactic fiction if you like: a town girl who has been ill, and is sent to stay for a year on her uncle's farm. There is no concealment of purpose: the chapters are bluntly titled January, February, and so on. Jane quite often asks appropriate questions. Yet, having watched the effect of the book on a child who had enjoyed all the Saville mystery-stories, and who possessed, if anything, rather less than the average interest in Nature, I feel that the purpose has been achieved.

To supplement such a book there is Agnes Allen's *The Story of the Village*, which is a local exploration from the human and historical angles. Again the device is transparent: a boy and his sister meet the village schoolmaster on the Downs, and obligingly bombard him with questions. Not only can he answer them: he can conjure up bygone villagers to deal with any awkward supplementaries. According to adult theory, children should hate the book. It is quite obvious they are being got at. They are being taught something. The pill looms grey beneath the thin gilt. But I have seen the book chosen to keep, after it had already been read, in preference to several stories offered at the same time.

I am not myself very partial to books in which representative characters from successive historical periods come back to earth for the instruction of boys and girls. *Puck of Pook's Hill* is the only one I can remember really enjoying; in the hands of other producers this sort of psychic pageantry is apt to be tiresome. It is not only the grave that yawns. Children clearly have more stomach for it, and Agnes Allen has certainly employed it to good purpose.

We are on safer ground when we turn to the story-biography. We may feel that the imaginative biographer is a doubtful ally of history when he writes for adults. There has been a great vogue for his books in recent years, for there is a class of intellectual snobs (mainly feminine, it must be pointed out with more candour than chivalry) who declare that they do not waste time on novels but read only biographies and memoirs. Such readers have no interest in footnotes, appendices and authorities. They want dogmatic statement, garnished with salacious innuendo. They are duly catered for. As the late John Palmer said of them, in that masterly life of Molière which demonstrates that wit and a respect for truth are not incompatible: 'It is a poor biographer who allows himself to be defeated by lack of evidence.' It would not be so bad if these writers would acknowledge, in a foreword to their fancies, that they lack complete omniscience; if they would emulate Froude's candour, who completed his contribution to Newman's *Lives of the Saints* with these words: 'I have said all that is known, and indeed a good deal more than is known, about the blessed St Neot.'

Grown-ups who boast of reading anything historical at all should be capable of some judgement. If the truth of a matter is not certain they should be told. They should not throw down the book in a pet if, at an exciting point in the narrative, the writer is compelled by intellectual honesty to call a halt and discuss questions of evidence or alternative hypotheses. Even in a vividly written popular work, which contains no new material, the reader should be given a brief general idea of the sources tapped.

Children cannot normally be expected to have this historical approach. By the time they are beginning to develop it, in the Sixth Form (if ever), they are ready for the adult books. Before that stage they need not biography, but story-biography.

The distinction is not between fact and fiction. The 'story-biographer' should be no less concerned with truth than his colleague writing for maturer minds. But, having established that truth in his own mind, he has to present it in an attractive and digestible form.

He knows (if he also writes pure fiction for children) that the young reader demands clear issues. There must be a plain, black-and-white conflict, resolved if not by an actual victory for the good, at least by a moral one. There must be a protagonist who, though not perfect, can command sympathy and admiration. The most odious creature who lives is a fit and necessary subject for adult biography, provided that he achieves eminence in some field – as such people almost invariably do. He cannot be the subject of a story-biography which children will enjoy; if he is of such historical importance that it is desirable to tell his story, he can best be introduced as the antagonist of some sympathetic character, who is sufficiently outstanding to take the title-role. We have not only to rule out the odious, but the mean and the dull – which again will exclude a large percentage of the world's notables. Children, it has been said, want flesh-and-blood heroes, not abstract ideals. There must be some sort of heroic streak (though it may run through a mass of human frailty) which claims the reader's admiration.

The biographer should not be afraid of the frailty. Too often the departed great have been held up for uncritical adulation. Authors forget they are telling a story, and write as though they were selling something. Take a man like Ralegh, an ideal biographical subject for children – colourful, rich in *coups de théâtre*, historically significant, and, may one add, remarkably free from those sexual skeletons-in-the-cupboard which make it hard or impossible to give children full-length portraits of most great men. The tale of Ralegh is incomprehensible if his faults are forgotten – his ambition, his vanity, his love of money, his capacity for sulking like a child – but they are faults within the sympathetic experience of the young reader. Perhaps, indeed, they will help in the process of identification.... There are only two difficulties in the theme (I speak with feeling, for I have had to face them), one being Ralegh's brutality in Ireland, which must be admitted, in honesty, yet which endangers his hold on the reader's sympathy as no other fault does; the second difficulty, of quite another sort, is the absence of data on Ralegh's boyhood. It is a sound principle that in these story-biographies a disproportionate space should be allotted to the subject's early years, so that the reader is better able to achieve imaginative identification. Ralegh, unlike Clive and Nelson, left no anecdotes to help us.

This persistent juvenile urge to identify oneself with the hero or heroine of the story imposes another necessity upon the biographer, which he will regret in direct ratio with his strength of conscience as a historian, but which (I think) he will have to bow to if he is to be widely read: he must from time to time presume to enter, and to beckon the reader after him, into the very mind of his subject. This is, historically speaking, most reprehensible. How much harm it actually does will depend on the intelligence of his guesses. But guess he must, at times. Youthful interest cannot be held indefinitely by a distant public figure, however heroic, seen above the heads of the crowd.

Dialogue may have to be invented. A children's story without dialogue is almost unthinkable, but heroes have seldom carried their Boswells into action with them. Even with Ralegh, though the State Papers enshrine so many of his brightest *mots*, we shall never be historically certain what he said to Bess Throckmorton when he, in his golden armour as Captain of the Guard, and she, arrayed as one of the Queen's ladies-in-waiting, whispered their plans for the secret wedding. But at this point the young reader will demand dialogue, and if the guesswork is good, Clio will utter scarcely a squeak of protest. She put up with a good deal more from Thucydides, who thought of the technique first.

It is not often that a really bad story-biography gets published. They are not obvious best-sellers, and depend very much on their ability to satisfy librarians and teachers. They involve research. In short, they are a poor proposition for the second-rate writer, who can earn twice as much in half the time by writing up a familiar formula in short lines of exclamatory dialogue. Why stew in the Bodleian when, by the simple process of letting the twins tether their ponies in the Abbey ruins, and search the secret passage till they find the jewels, one can knock off a really popular book inside the month?

Fortunately, some of our best writers of juvenile fiction have felt otherwise. L. A. G. Strong produced *Henry of Agincourt* and *The Man Who Asked Questions*, the story of Socrates; Lorna Lewis has written of Nansen (as has Aubrey de Selincourt) and Leonardo da Vinci; Carola Oman, whose double-decker *Nelson* puts her among the best of the living adult biographers, has depicted King Alfred for the young reader; Kitty Barne wrote *Elizabeth Fry*.

Eleanor Doorly did not write fiction. Her biographies of the French scientists, *The Insect Man*, *The Microbe Man* and *The Radium Woman* won her a specially honoured niche. Robert

Gibbings' decorations probably helped a good deal to attract children in the first instance, since the themes were not superficially appealing to the majority of them.

What they did for the scientists, Elizabeth Ripley has done for numerous artists from Botticelli to Picasso, and Opal Wheeler and Sybil Deucher (as joint-authors) with Mary Greenwalt (as illustrator) similarly for the musicians. *Sebastian Bach: The Boy from Thuringia, Joseph Haydn: The Merry Little Peasant* and *Mozart: The Wonder Boy* were the first of a now-familiar series. Opal Wheeler and Mary Greenwalt have since produced volumes about Beethoven, Handel and Stephen Foster. They have big pages and bold, lively pictures. The music, scored for the piano, is introduced naturally in the course of the story, sometimes just a few bars, sometimes whole pieces that are within the compass of the young pianist. They are thus something more than biographies: they are a direct stimulus to piano-playing.

These books can be enjoyed rather sooner than the Doorly biographies. A more exact equivalent to, say, *The Microbe Man*, is C. H. Abrahall's *Prelude*, which deals with the early life of Eileen Joyce, from her Tasmanian childhood (with much emphasis on a lovable pet kangaroo named Twink) to her first appearance in the Albert Hall. The biographer of a living person labours under certain disadvantages, but in this case there is one great compensation – the subject is available to answer questions about those earliest years, so interesting to the child-reader, when no one else was noticing. This is a good 'struggling-career' story, with some of that quality of inspiration which juvenile biography is intended to supply. And once more there is a distinguished illustrator, Anna Zinkeisen, a friend of the subject and not likely (one would think) to forfeit that friendship as a result of these drawings. They are printed in black and petunia, a scheme which enhances their charm, but makes it impossible to reproduce an example which would do them justice.

The careers of a ballet-dancer and of an author are represented, respectively, by Gladys Malvern's life of Pavlova, *Dancing Star*, and *The Story of Hans Andersen* by Esther Meynell. It would be an excellent thing if every library had a shelf of such books, each dealing with a different vocation and some of them emphasizing that romantic struggles are not the exclusive preserve of artists and scientists. Such a shelf would include autobiographies like Patricia Lynch's *A Storyteller's Childhood*, and grouped shorter life-stories such as Eleanor Farjeon's *Ten Saints*, Elfrida Vipont's *Sparks Among the Stubble*, and Amabel Williams-Ellis's *Good Citizens*.

Certain persons – Queen Elizabeth, Florence Nightingale, Drake, Nelson – will probably continue to attract rather more than their fair share of attention. One of these ultra-familiar figures is well treated in Mildred Criss's *Mary Stuart: Young Queen of Scots*. I had always stood firm against that feline monarch's notorious charm. I had watched unmoved, over and over again, her interminable last hours re-enacted by amateurs in drama festivals. Mildred Criss, limiting herself to the early period which ends with the girl-widow's farewell to France, produced a book which won me over.

Let us end with a curiosity.

We have looked at stories which were designed to teach history and geography, Nature Study and how to pick a career. *The Avion My Uncle Flew*, by the American writer Cyrus Fisher, is an experiment in teaching French.

Johnny, who tells the story, has to spend his convalescence with a French uncle in 'a little no 'count French village'. As a one-hundred-per-cent American boy, he has a highly developed resistance to all languages but his own. The theme is the gradual weakening of this resistance as he comes to see the inconveniences involved. Odd French words are introduced into the story chapter by chapter, and one or two very elementary grammatical points are clarified along with the other mysteries of the plot, which deals with the attempt to steal the glider his uncle has invented. This linguistic infiltration proceeds stealthily until on page 250 the French words capture the position, and hold it unchallenged to 'La Fin' on page 253. This climax is all very fine and would gratify any language-teacher. It is the long struggle while the issue is still undecided – when French and English, not to mention American, grapple within the same sentence ('That ended French leçons for this jour', page 94) – which the schoolmaster might feel justified in describing as bloody in the extreme.

Cyrus Fisher is a lively writer in this holiday-mystery style. His educational motive was admirable, his conception original, but—

It's a good holiday-mystery, anyhow.

CHAPTER SIX

The Comic and the Blood

'WOULD you like one of my comics to read?' my
landlady's daughter inquired hospitably one day
during World War II. I answered tactfully, but on
renewed pressure explained that it was some twenty-five years
since I had read a comic, and I had in the meantime developed
other literary preferences. The girl looked at me incredulously.
'We've had ever so many soldiers staying here before you,'
she said, 'and I never knew one that didn't like comics. Not one!'
I must have looked equally incredulous, for she went on: 'I
always send them to Daddy in India when I've finished with
them, and *he* loves them, and he says they go all round the
hospitals.' Daddy, I happened to know, was a college-trained
pharmacist.

No survey of juvenile fiction would be complete without a
glance at this mass of periodical literature which has such a
remarkable hold not only on children but also (as the war
showed to many others besides myself) on a number of adults.
This, after all, is the fiction which the child buys. 'Our aim,'
I was told by the leading firm of publishers in this field, 'is to
produce papers which will be bought *by* the child, not *for* him;
or, if they are bought *for* him, then at his own insistence.' Their
success is conspicuous. Pessimists declare that it doesn't matter
what we put into our books because the literature of the
juvenile masses is the comic and the blood. That is going too
far. It is, partly for financial reasons, what they buy: it is by no
means all that they read. Children's libraries are increasing and
improving; so are school-libraries, either independently or in
association with the local children's librarian. Local authorities,
following a lead originally given by the National Book League,
hold exhibitions and lectures, film-shows and competitions, in

heir drive for a higher membership. You have only to walk
ito a typical children's library and see the rush of borrowers
fter school, or take out some first-class story from the shelf and
)ok at the issue-record. It has probably been out forty or
fty times, though there may be several copies of the same title
1 the library. It is as misleading to exaggerate the monopoly
·f the comic as to leave its wide popularity out of our reckoning.

Juvenile magazines are almost as old as books. One ran for a
ear, under that name, in 1788. By 1822 another, *The Youth's
Monthly Visitor*, was finding it necessary to protest against the
:heap and ephemeral publications of the day'. It proposed to
ittend to the solid improvement of the youth of both sexes'
·y 'combining instruction with rational amusement', by ex-
·ounding the sciences and by 'Moral Tales, Anecdotes, Poetical
ixtracts, etc., etc.' It lasted eighteen months.

A more successful effort was *Chatterbox*, founded in 1866
·y a Derby clergyman who 'hated to see errand boys of fourteen
·r so reading nothing but (as he called it outright) "blood and
hunder".' Then there was *The Prize*, against which Ruskin
ulminated for its mawkish sentiment and doggerel verse. Such
·apers, he complained, had 'no lightheartedness, no joy, no
·reedom'.

In 1879 came The *Boy's Own Paper*, perhaps the only English
·uvenile periodical which has ever really succeeded in combining
·noral policy, good writing and genuine popularity. In its
·olden dawn the *B.O.P.* offered the fiction of Kingston and
/erne, Baines Reed and Ballantyne; Captain Webb wrote on
·wimming and Dr Grace on cricket. A year later the girls were
·rovided with the *G.O.P.*, never so influential, but popular
·or a generation or two, until it changed its name to *Heiress*,
·ecame just another young women's magazine, and quickly
·ied. Stephen King-Hall's *Mine* had a brief bright life in the
·ineteen-thirties. Now the standard of quality is best upheld
·y *Elizabethan*, founded as *Collins Magazine for Boys and Girls*.
The danger with such papers is that, revolting against blood
·nd thunder, they sometimes rush to the other extreme, putting

in too many informative articles about the ballet and the symphony, and too many Post-Impressionist reproductions. The result is a magazine received with glee in North Oxford and indifference in the North of England. Not that a modest circulation is to be despised, so long as it is enough to keep a paper afloat; after all, for the best part of its two centuries English juvenile literature has been produced and sustained by a middle-class minority. But the advent of universal literacy and Northcliffe journalism made a mass-circulation possible; it produced Sexton Blake and Billy Bunter, and their successors today. It is with them that we must primarily concern ourselves.

While travelling years ago through several Midland towns I made a point of buying all the different comics I saw. The first thing I noticed was that there was no monopoly in this field - the *Sun* and the *Comet*, issued by a small firm in Manchester, were as much in evidence as the *Rainbow* and *Film Fun*. So much for the prevalent illusion that some miraculous change of heart in the Fleetway House could transform the juvenile press over night. My second discovery was that these papers change much more than might be imagined from George Orwell's famous essay on the subject, though his estimate of their basic value was - and is - still sound. The *Magnet* and the *Gem* no longer existed. Billy Bunter, though he had achieved the dignity of book form, survived elsewhere only in a corner of *Knock-out* and as a comic strip in that paper. This last tribute was shared by Sexton Blake and Tinker. The *Rainbow* I recognized with sentimental pleasure; it had changed less than I had in the many years since we had met. Tiger Tim and the Bruin Boys, bless them, were still sliding down the stairs on a tea-tray, and doing unlikely things with giant snowballs. Sing Hi and Sing Lo were up to the old antics, Bluebell was having the usual adventures. Perhaps I was prejudiced, but the *Rainbow* seemed to stand out a cut above most comics. There was no American slang: even the cowboys talked passable English. Only in the historical short story did I note the invariable romantic bias, which is not confined to comics and to which I shall revert in another chapter.

'Cavalier!' he answered promptly.
The little girl smiled.
'I thought you looked too nice to be a
     Roundhead.'

Today, alas, the *Rainbow* is as extinct as the *Sun* and *Comet*.

There is a considerable difference in the get-up of various
papers, and it is only fair to stress this, since adult critics are apt
to lump them all together without examining them. They are
all supposed to combine crude illustration with type so small
and bad that it ruins the eyesight. One publisher admitted to
me that the type was smaller than was desirable, but that owing
to cost of paper it was impossible to give value for money
otherwise. 'You must remember,' he said, 'that the children's
eyesight is generally better than that of the grown-ups who are
criticizing.' The temptation to ask, 'for how long?', was considerable.

There is no threat to the eyesight in the *Beano* and the *Beezer*,
representatives of a large class of comics which do not tax the
concentration powers of their public with more than about
four lines of print at a time and allow their strip-stories to be
told largely in single words and ejaculations. 'Thud', 'Hiya',
'Grr', 'Oowooh', 'Ooyah', 'Heh! Heh!', 'W-W-Whu-u-up!' and
a score of other ingenious variants are scattered over almost
every page, all printed large and often entirely in capital letters.
It is illuminating to compare these strips with those appearing
in papers such as *Eagle, Girl* and *Boys' World*, where the text
(like the art work) is infinitely better and there is no great
reliance on onomatopoeia. These papers also print short stories
and articles. The typography, and the production generally,
now an advance on anything available in this field a few years
ago, and we should be grateful to that dynamic Anglican
clergyman, the Rev. Marcus Morris, who set new standards
if founding *Eagle* in 1950 and doing what editors had assured
me only a year or two earlier was impossible. Even under its
founder, *Eagle* always represented a compromise. It had to pay,
often went further than some of us would have wished in its

desperate determination to be popular. But it survived, and i
probably at the time of writing the most sought-after children'
weekly in the country – I write with feeling, after scouring
bookstalls in vain for current issues and having eventually to
order in advance. Despite the wide circulation of *Eagle* and on
or two other comics of comparable quality, the bulk of children'
reading in this field is much closer to the *Beano* and *Beezer* level

M. McLeish, writing in *Junior Bookshelf*, once compared
pile of comics with 'a whole group of pictures produced b
children themselves in their earlier and most creative years'
and added that 'one perceives at once the difference between
creative imagination and sophisticated unrealism'. It is true
that one's abiding impression is of mediocrity relieved only b
the damnably bad. This is a serious state of affairs, for, as w
have seen from our discussion of picture-books, the child'
taste in art is susceptible to every influence.

Turning to the text we are struck by the recurrence of stoc
themes. 'Inter-planetary journeys,' I noted in 1948, 'Tarzan
stories ("Wild Boy" in *Beano*, "Jungle Lord" in the *Comet* an
"Saki the Leopard Boy" in *Knock-out*), Inca treasure and los
cities of all kinds, Robin Hood, and the Mounties are the mos
common. Verne, Wells, Conan Doyle, Rider Haggard an
Rice Burroughs left behind them an inexhaustible store c
ideas, and there seems no attempt to think of any others.' Fiftee
years later a specimen half-dozen comics indicate little chang
Beezer has 'Jungle Boy' on a desert island, *Boys' World* show
Tarzan in India. The same issue of *Boys' World* has a 'terrib
monster, the legendary Sea Ape', living on 'the mysteriou
Island of Groans', but the *Eagle*'s 'Beast in Loch Craggon
though equally terrible in aspect, is depicted with the imag
nation and humanity characteristic of this paper's policy. 'Perhap
Jamie was right,' says the hero's father. 'The beast only attacl
to defend itself!' And the following week's instalment
announced as 'Jamie's Quest to Save the Monster'. Scienc
fiction, as is to be expected, holds its place. 'Is Exhibit "X" tryin
to enslave the human race?' asks *Boys' World*. 'Only John Brod
science investigator of the *Daily Newsflash*, is aware of th

danger. For, with his ultrasonic hearing, he is not affected by the hypnotic sounds "X" emits . . .' Simultaneously, if we are to believe the *Beezer*, 'in two rooms only a few miles apart, two groups of men discussed the strange, sponge-like weeds that had descended on Britain from outer space. To Professor Bill Masters, head of the Rocketry Research Establishment at Hartford Moor, the iron-eating sponges were the gravest danger ever to threaten Britain. But to Nat Brooker and his gang of crooks these same sponges were a key – a key to every safe in the country.' Meanwhile (on the back page of the same issue) 'deep in the snow wastes of the Purple Planet, the Silver family stood helpless as a horde of howling Ice-men swept up the slope. Not ten minutes before, the three space explorers had escaped from these same warriors when a giant gull had attacked their cliff castle.' *Eagle* has its most popular perennial character, Dan Dare, landing in a new spaceship 'on a floating island on the planet of Meit'. Only *Girl*, catering for feminine fantasies, is consistently down-to-earth with such themes as modelling in New York, becoming a pop singer or ballet-dancer, or travelling to Australia by scooter.

There is little to suggest that deep-laid political conspiracy of which some editors and publishers have felt themselves to be unjustly and ridiculously accused in the last paragraph of George Orwell's essay. I doubt if he ever meant all they thought he meant – that the ideology of comics was solemnly laid down by 'Lord Camrose and his colleagues' and enforced by directives from on high, though such things are familiar enough in the newspaper world and there is nothing inherently impossible in the idea. I am assured, and am prepared to believe, that there is no such direction; but I am not so sure that if a particular editor began to print a new type of story, building up a different sort of hero – a Spanish Loyalist in 1936, say – he might not hear the crack of the whip. So far as I know, such an experiment has never been tried, and I doubt if it will be.

There has probably been more searching criticism of comics than of children's books. Apart from George Orwell's trenchant onslaught there have been some severe things said by Berwick

Sayers ('they destroy the sense of beauty which should come from books and they are obviously destructive of eyesight'), by A. J. Jenkinson and by the New Zealander, W. J. Scott, whose chapter in his *Reading, Film and Radio Tastes of High School Boys and Girls* should be studied by all concerned. In the circumstances it seemed fair, when undertaking this survey, to solicit the opinions of the accused. I accordingly approached two large-scale firms and two small ones, saying that I should appreciate 'a brief statement of how you interpret your social responsibility and how you consider your publications fit into the educational fabric of the country, what tendencies you seek to encourage and discourage in your choice of fiction, and so on. I shall assume unless told otherwise that I may quote you verbatim . . .'

One small firm did not reply. The publishers of the *Wizard, Hotspur*, and other papers wrote:

> We are interested to hear of your work in connection with the children's reading. We do not feel, however, that we could discuss our business methods with an outside person and accordingly we are not in a position to give you any information.

Mr J. B. Allen, then publishing the *Sun* and *Comet*, was more helpful.

> The policy I try to pursue is that there shall be no 'Deadwood Dick' rubbish and I insist that all murder shall be cut out from stories and pictures.
>
> Recently I have learned an object lesson in catering for children, and in the 'Sun' ran on the front page in serial form 'Swiss Family Robinson'. I regret to say that we dropped in circulation about 7,000 per issue. We received hundreds of letters demanding that we take off 'Swiss Family' and put on a thriller, and this I had to do to save the paper. . . .
>
> If you are going to get to the children you must publish stories of adventure. If you do not, then they will not read them. I ask my writers and artists to try and work in some educational value. In the 'Cruise of the Cormorant' the writer often worked in a bit of history where he made the ship call. The difficulty here is that

very few artists and writers know anything about the history of the places they try to visualize.

I have taken a deep interest in children for many years, and was for a time connected with schools. To get them to read anything of a serious nature is a problem. The only way I can think of is to give them what they will read, and in some way work in that educational factor.

This letter was still very much in my mind when, in response to a courteous invitation from the last of the firms, I went to visit the Amalgamated Press as it then was.

I found here no fumbling, well-meaning experiments in education. A frank admission of purely commercial motive was coupled with a quite sincere pride in the tradition of the house for providing 'clean healthy reading'. (I speak, of course, for the two representatives with whom I talked, separately, for well over an hour. As one remarked, for all he knew the building might contain Communists and bigamists, but so long as they did not put their views into *Comic Cuts* or *Knock-out*, they were welcome to them.) There had never, I was assured, been any ideological directives from above. It had never occurred to anybody in pre-Orwell days that the comic paper could possibly be used as a propaganda weapon and it had not been so used since. The only attempt to influence the reader was on certain non-controversial moral questions such as kindness to animals and Road Safety. The only taboos were on themes like murder and snakes, which gave children the horrors. Having used snakes in two Children's Hour short stories myself, I hung my head with due penitence.

Such a publishing group does not, like Mr Allen, receive hundreds of letters in protest against an ill-judged experiment. It knows its job too well. Its aim is to give the child-public what it wants, and it has been doing this for so many years now that it makes no serious miscalculations. It has its finger on the juvenile pulse. If the public has ceased to care for the *Magnet* and *Gem*, no sentimental consideration will save those former favourites. A company like this does not follow changes in public taste – it is too deft for that, it anticipates them. But it makes no attempt to lead them, any more than my shadow leads me when it happens to fall in front of me as I walk. As W. J. Scott remarks:

> The great and sustained popularity of the bloods confronts the teacher of English with an acutely difficult problem. At every age he will have in his class a considerable number of pupils who are not mentally and emotionally developed enough to get much from the literature he asks them to read and discuss. Its picture of human nature in action is too complex for them, separated by too great a gap from the reading which deeply moves them. Here again the heavy downward pressure of our commercial culture frustrates much of the teacher's efforts. It is no concern of the Amalgamated Press and the other firms to help boys and girls to grow up by progressively altering the proportions of compensation and experience for each stage of their development. This would mean publishing two or three magazines instead of one as now, a less profitable undertaking.

These men are journalists; they do not claim to be politicians, educationists or psychologists, save perhaps in the jargon sense of 'sales-psychology'. Their intentions are excellent. They would not publish anything they would not take home for their own children to read. The trouble is that they are unaware of the subtler effects of their fiction. That is why a great gulf of misunderstanding separated them from George Orwell. They know they mean well, they know that they are not operating a deliberate policy of any kind, but they do not realize that the mere exclusion of murder, snakes and sex does not in itself produce healthy literature. To quote W. J. Scott again:

> A child's reading, it has been suggested, is done to get either compensation or experience or both. These stories supply little but compensation. The characters are merely channels for boyish fantasies that help to restore a balance disturbed by difficulties of adjustment to the concerns of daily life . . . The plots move with the ease of a well-organized day-dream.

And once more:

An acceptance with such enthusiasm of a representation of human beings in action that is so patently false must tend to create some misunderstanding in the mind of the young reader of the nature and motives of human behaviour. Further it compels him to lead a dual existence, using a part in his energy in an excessive, emotional participation in a life of fantasy at a time when he needs so much to understand and grapple with the real world. Granted that it is still necessary for him to withdraw sometimes from the real world into one of fantasy, it is of great importance that the experience given in the fantasy should be of good quality, indirectly extending his understandings of reality.

Which deserves to be read and re-read, not only by those concerned with the humble blood and comic, but by many who consider themselves 'high-class' book-publishers and authors.

What about style? It varies. The worst English comes in the captions. There is that grating use of 'like' for 'as': 'Old Lou's brain holds ideas like a sieve holds water. Just like an elephant never forgets, so Lou never remembers.' There is the Americanism: 'Uncle's first remark sure gave Bud food for thought.' There is the sniggering facetiousness of: ' T' other day she accompanied him on a fishing expedish and Joe had just dropped the tiddlers a line when Susie caught something. Nunno, not with a fish-hook, chums.' The same strip contains 'unforch', 'peepers', 'thusly', 'the wetness', 'shocka', 'figure out', 'tootled', 'prezactly' and 'invite' (for invitation). All these examples came from an issue of *Film Fun*, published by the Amalgamated Press. In *Knock-out* we can study the deliberate misspelling joke: 'At larst Ethelbert hit on a crarfty skeem for gathering grub.' The English teacher does not get much more assistance from such publications as D. C. Thomson's *Dandy*, with its pathetic doggerel:

> The gang have had a rotten deal
> For they don't even get a meal.
> Young Patsy sits there with a smile—
> Her extra bath was sure worth while.

Berwick Sayers, trying to be scrupulously fair to the comic, has suggested that it may lead children on to better things, from Sexton Blake to Sherlock Holmes, and from Tiger Tim to Beatrix Potter, Winnie-the-Pooh and the *Jungle Books*. Even he will hardly suggest that *Dandy* is the first step on the road to *The Waste Land*.

The standard of English in the stories is usually much better. Berwick Sayers recalls one description of a London fog in a Sexton Blake story which had the quality of *Bleak House*. That is quite likely. Dickens, great popular entertainer that he was, shared many characteristics with the anonymous purveyors of the blood. *The House of Thrills*, published in *Film Fun*, has the over-written theatrical quality of bad Dickens:

> The flickering yellow light of six candles illumined the handsome, clean-cut features of John Pentonville as he sat in a sombre, cobweb-hung room in ancient Gaunt House.
>
> Clad in faultless evening clothes, the wounded ex-wing commander looked strikingly out of place in that grim setting. Gaunt House had the reputation of being haunted. People living in the neighbourhood hesitated before passing the sinister old house, and dogs slunk by with bared fangs as though conscious of its baleful influence.

Like George Orwell, passing the Fleetway House . . .

This extract, with its monotonous hammering home of its point – flickering, sombre, cobweb, ancient, grim, sinister, baleful (even the proper names, Gaunt and Pentonville, are evocative) – and its cliché-laden hero, the handsome clean-cut wounded ex-R.A.F. type in his faultless evening clothes, is a fair sample. The story which follows is in this case almost disappointingly credible, apart from one unlikely but essential coincidence, and the morality is impeccable. The style may blunt the literary taste of the young reader and render it insensitive to subtler flavours, but the grammar is as faultless as the evening dress. Most of these stories are poor stuff, but there is little perceptible difference between them and dozens which attain the respectability of publication in books and annuals.

The real 'blood' of yesteryear, so amusingly surveyed in E. S. Turner's *Boys Will Be Boys* – the novelette of twenty to forty thousand words, bringing each fortnight a new adventure of an old character – is now of little significance, for its place has been largely taken by the more lurid of the paperbacks, all smoking guns and unbuttoned bosoms, which being classed by courtesy as adult reading fall outside our scope. Sexton Blake, though surviving till 1963, long ago ceased to be the national figure he once was, and will soon no doubt be almost as dim a memory as his rival detective, Nelson Lee, or Buffalo Bill in so far as he was depicted in the *Buffalo Bill Library*. It would be the same with Frank Richards' schoolboy characters had they still depended on novelette-publication, but television gave Billy Bunter a fresh lease of life and in due course the belated dignity of a hardback edition. The feminine equivalent of the 'blood' – with the accent on romance rather than violence – has perhaps held its ground a little more successfully, but as the natural climax to each story is a happy-ever-after marriage, it is not surprising that these 'libraries' have not established memorable recurrent characters like those which used so to fascinate the boys.

Annuals, since we have mentioned them, may be dealt with summarily here, for in all but format they closely resemble periodical literature. This is a natural consequence of the old practice of rebinding magazines like the *B.O.P.*, *Chums*, and *Chatterbox*, and selling them at Christmas. Although nowadays most of the annuals consist of new or at least completely re-arranged material, their contents are similar to those of the periodicals. Each level of taste has its annuals to correspond, but efforts to provide something outstandingly good, as in Jonathan Cape's *Adventure and Discovery*, primarily for boys, and *Discovery and Romance* for girls, seem unable to continue for long. All the considerations so far discussed in this chapter apply to the annual, and no separate survey is necessary.

There can be little doubt that the periodicals read by English children are still, on the whole, a poor lot. They entertain, but in few cases do they do more. If we acquit them of any consciously evil direction, we can hardly acquit them of bad artistic and typographical standards, unintentional but no less unhealthy psychological influences and English which shades down from the mediocre-but-grammatical to the crude yowlings of the gutter. Can anything be done?

With the good will of the publishers, it could. Are they really in the market for better pictures and stories? Are they prepared to believe competent authorities that the encouragement of excessive fantasy-life is bad – and then tell their contributors that it must be cut out, along with murder and cruelty to animals?

The pioneer work of Marcus Morris and others has shown just how much – and how little, in some ways – it is possible to achieve. Periodicals and annuals must always by their nature constitute a 'package deal', made up primarily of commodities known to attract a given group of young readers – which, as production costs increase, needs to be ever larger. In a Britain where, for newspapers, a mere million circulation means bankruptcy, even the *Eagle* dares not soar too high above the mediocre and conventional. A generation ago economic conditions allowed a magazine like the *B.O.P.* to take a book-length story and offer it, with other features, in just two gigantic instalments of 25,000 words each. Those conditions are unlikely to return. The story-teller who has something to say and needs a little space in which to explain himself – above all, the writer who wants to do something new – must find expression in books, where fortunately it is still possible to cater for a minority public. He will seldom find much artistic satisfaction in writing fiction for magazines and annuals.

CHAPTER SEVEN

Tough as They Come

'GOVERNING bodies and managers of schools have been far too niggardly in supplying good books in their schools for general adventure story and exciting reading,' said the Parliamentary Secretary to the Ministry of Education in 1947. 'It is appalling that we as a nation are so mean in supplying this essential tool of learning. We spent £500,000,000 in 1946 in gambling and pools – and governing bodies of grammar schools and sub-committees of local education authorities think it is marvellous to grant £50 a year for the school library.'

No writer of adventure stories will lack sympathy with this view – though some may blink momentarily to find their books promoted to the status of educational tools, and essential ones at that. Would it be ungracious to speculate how long it was since the Parliamentary Secretary had found time, amid the preoccupations of political life, to handle one of these tools? And were the conference members, who (we trust) applauded his recommendations, any more up to date in their knowledge? Were they merely carried away, for the moment, by boyhood memories of Ballantyne? What did they, and the speaker, wish the scholar to 'learn' from the adventure story? These questions are asked in all sincerity and goodwill. Spend the fifty pounds. But, in the name of education, spend it carefully. Make sure that the stories do not teach what you do not want the boy to learn.

The English adventure story is, in its way, one of our supreme contributions to world literature. Though our nineteenth-century novelists may have lagged behind the French and Russians, in the adolescent field the writer in English (we must extend the definition to cover Americans like Fenimore Cooper) has had a monopoly which scarcely any foreign author except

Jules Verne has seriously challenged until modern times. Our tradition is rooted in Defoe. The French acknowledged that when they invented the useful word, *robinsonnade*. Many such *robinsonnades* were written on the Continent: where are they now, except for the *Swiss Family*, which is poor stuff compared with *Crusoe*? Marryat and Fenimore Cooper carried on the tradition. Just a hundred years ago it came to a sudden blossoming, with Mayne Read starting to write in the late eighteen-forties, with Kingston's *Peter the Whaler* coming out in 1851, Kingsley's *Westward Ho!* (intended originally for adults) in 1855, and Ballantyne's *The Young Fur-Traders* a year later.

The importance of this period is underlined by Harvey Darton. 'The true novelty in these books,' he writes, 'was the absence of any appeal to a dogmatic religious belief, or any *open* theory of conduct or education. The belief and the theory were at last kept inside the authors' minds. The heroes are shown as praying, as trusting in God, as stout Britons with a sense of honour, honesty and duty . . . but [those qualities] are not the dominating, purposeful, obvious cause of the book's existence.'

The popularity of these stories in their own day is something which we can now hardly imagine. The publisher was still often a bookseller, and on the morning when a new Ballantyne came out the street would be blocked with fashionable carriages. 'I wonder sometimes,' wrote Edgar Osborne in *Junior Bookshelf*, 'whether British people generally, or historians in particular, fully realize the debt we owe to these boys' writers of the nineteenth century who did so much to stimulate the spirit of adventure amongst young people, many of whom went overseas and did much towards building up our present Commonwealth of Nations.'

And how does it strike critics abroad? Paul Hazard summed up the implicit message of these books with Gallic irony: 'Love your country . . . Its absolute superiority over all the other nations of the world is indisputable. This superiority must be considered a dogma established once and for all . . . Do not waste your time refuting those who contradict you, since no one would do so if he were in his right mind.'

Is that attitude of mind one of the objectives we are to seek when financing school libraries? Oh, come, let us be fair, you say. Hazard had Henty weighed up perhaps, but Henty died in 1902. Surely the old formula, 1 Englishman equals 2 Frenchmen equals 4 Germans equals *n* dagoes, Chinks, niggers and lesser breeds generally, is not one that modern writers would work to?

They are less blatant about it, certainly. Their nationalism is rather more subtle, but it remains.

'We have no Ballantyne today,' I wrote in 1948. 'The adventure story has slumped in status. A modern Stevenson would not write about galleons – it would be *infra dig*. Fanciful, whimsical "nonsense", by all means. Several factual cruises round Skye, if you like. But nothing so vulgar as the Spanish Main. First-class writers and artists seldom stoop so low.'

Since those words were written there has been some improvement. Writers of the calibre of Lawrence Durrell, Richard Church, and P. H. Newby have contributed the odd book, and others, more primarily children's authors, have created (or consolidated) high reputations – Richard Armstrong and Captain Frank Knight with their sea-stories, the many-sided Ian Serraillier, the American Armstrong Sperry, and the French René Guillot, prolific in production and as lush in language as the jungle about which he loves to write, mingling brilliance of imagination with occasional lapses into absurdity. But still no one enjoys the respect once accorded to Ballantyne and Henty. Few but the writers themselves realize that the 'yarn' (as it is so often patronizingly described) has the same potentialities as the fantasy so dear to the intelligentsia. John Cowper Powys knew it, when he wrote in *The Pleasures of Literature*: 'Not the most thrilling tale of adventure but, on its own particular level and in its own peculiar vein, offers some commentary, emphasizes some significant fact, or theory, or feeling, which in its special connection, and in its own tone, accent and measure, criticizes our life upon earth.' Until that is admitted, the adventure-story will continue to be under-valued, and it will not attract enough authors of the top flight.

In sales and popularity I imagine the foremost English writer in this field is still Captain W. E. Johns, creator of 'Biggles', 'Gimlet', and even a feminine counterpart to 'Biggles', known as 'Worrals of the W.A.A.F.' Once, at a remote wayside station on the Hardangervidda, I found them selling 'Biggles' in Norwegian. I could well believe the author when he wrote in 1948: 'Even with the paper shortage my books are still published at a rate of more than a quarter of a million a year. They appear in nearly every European language and three Oriental ones. Make a note that these countries are trying to educate their youth to the British way of life. They have told me so . . . It is curious that the only English-speaking country in which my books do not sell well is America. An American publisher accounted for this by saying my stuff was "too God-damned British". Put what construction you like on that.'

I had asked Captain Johns why he wrote for children. 'First of all,' he answered, 'for the entertainment of my reader. That is, I give boys what they want, not what their elders and betters think they ought to read. I teach at the same time, under a camouflage. Juveniles are keen to learn, but the educational aspect must not be too obvious or they become suspicious of its intention. I teach a boy to be a man, for without that essential qualification he will never be anything. I teach sportsmanship according to the British idea. One doesn't need blood and thunder to do that. In more than forty novels about my hero Biggles he has only once struck a man, and that was a matter of life and death. I teach that decent behaviour wins in the end as a natural order of things. I teach the spirit of team-work, loyalty to the Crown, the Empire, and to rightful authority.'

In a later passage he continued: 'Today, more than ever before, the training of the juvenile mind is important. The adult author has little hope of changing the outlook, politics, or way of life, of his reader, whose ideas are fixed. The brain of a boy is flexible, still able to absorb. It can be twisted in any direction. A born hero-worshipper, he adores his heroes, and what they do he will do, so upon the actions of his heroes will his own character be formed. I know from my fan mail how true this is. Upon us, who cater for him at the most impressionable age of his life, rests a responsibility which has been perceived by at least one political party. To them I must give credit for working out that in four or five years' time these readers will be voters. Biggles, therefore, may have some bearing on the future of the country. But he will remain Biggles. He isn't interested in politics. He stands for something higher. Boys who read of his exploits may be able to tell you what this is.'

It is to be hoped that even the adults reading this paragraph have still sufficiently absorbent brains to take in its highly interesting implications. Meanwhile, let us adopt the suggestion in the final sentence. What can the boys tell us? Paul Harlen speaking, fourteen years old, in *Junior Bookshelf*: 'Biggles seems to me a true Britisher. He always fights for right against might . . . Biggles is a born leader of men, a man to look up to with admiration. He is, in fact, the type of man that I would like to be. The supporting characters, Ginger and Algy, back Biggles up in everything he does and do not argue too much. Their chief virtue is that they hero-worship Biggles . . . The villains are entirely different. It is easy to hate them.' There could hardly be a more eloquent tribute to a writer's success in achieving a desired effect.

Several points arise from the foregoing statements. There is the nationalist bias of the adventure story. Closely related to this is the attitude towards foreigners it encourages and the picture it presents of foreign countries. There is the thorny psychological question of violence. And there is the cult of the hero.

'The instant the first native burst from cover Frank opened fire, shooting with an accuracy born of long practice on game,' wrote Wilfrid Robertson in *The Missing Legatee*, soon after the Second World War, 'You're a disgrace to your own colour! Faugh! You make me sick, you rotten swine,' declares a character in the story, in which the local Africans are referred to as 'savages' and 'niggers'. The author knew the country.

His story is quite exciting, though it involves one of those familiar quests for a large legacy, 'by the terms of their rich uncle's will', and has one of those morally dishonest denouements, by which the villain obligingly walks into an animal-trap at the finish, and saves hero and author alike from awkward decisions on how to deal with him. Still, the first-hand picture of East Africa would justify a place in the school library were it not for the racial attitude. It is not aggressive: just implicit. That calm shooting-down of natives recalls Robinson Crusoe's methodical accountancy – do you remember?

> 3 killed at our first shot from the tree.
> 2 killed at the next shot.
> 2 killed by Friday in the boat.
> 2 killed by ditto, of those at first wounded.
> 1 killed by ditto in the wood.
> 3 killed by the Spaniard.
> 4 killed, being found dropped here and there of their wounds, or killed by Friday in his chase of them.
> 4 escaped in the boat, whereof one wounded, if not dead.
> 21 in all.

No one but a crank would wish to censor Defoe. The adventure story of today, however, should reflect the somewhat altered attitude of the late twentieth century, and the school library should supplement, not contradict, what is taught in the classroom.

Nowadays we presumably want our children to think of men and women, whatever their nationality and colour, as individuals rather than as types. But most writers of adventure-stories find type-casting easier, as film-directors do. So in the old kind of story we have the funny Frenchman and the guttural German, the oily Italian and the sinister Chinese. Indians talk in voluble *babu* English, while Red Indians confine their remarks to a grunted 'How?' Natives – a term which implies a dark skin and semi-nudity – are 'loyal' in so far as they co-operate with the white man, and 'treacherous' when they do not.

It would be stupid to deny that certain rough national

generalizations are possible, and indeed inevitable. But in so far as the story-writer allows himself to introduce 'typical' foreigners, it is up to him to see that they are closer to the truth than they have been in the past. The French zest for civilized living, the German capacity for organization, the distinctive dignity of the Spanish peasant however poor . . . these are, up to a point, valid generalizations, and can be used to promote international understanding and good-will. It is important to get away, once for all, from stock villains like Fu Manchu.

Fortunately there are many influences at work to correct these false impressions. The modern child has far more personal experience of foreigners, in his own country and increasingly in theirs. Television continually reminds him of the common humanity linking us all. And in the field of children's literature itself we have more and more translations from the best of the contemporary European authors – books like *Avalanche* by Rutgers van der Loeff, a Dutch author writing about Switzerland and introducing the Pestalozzi villagers, *The Orphans of Simitra* (a Greek earthquake story by Paul-Jacques Bonzon), Paul Berna's *A Hundred Million Francs*, Maria Gleit's *Child of China* (translated from the German), Michel-Aimé Baudouy's *Children of the Marshes* (set on a bull-farm near Seville), and a number of others. We have also a mass of our own stories, good, bad and indifferent, about British children on the Continent, in which the 'natives' are usually depicted in a reasonably truthful way. The chief snag is that such stories, like the foreign translations, seldom fall into the 'tough-as-they-come' class and therefore do not reach the boy who wants stronger meat than a credible everyday setting, with boys and girls as main characters, is likely to provide.

One nation the British child will increasingly need to understand as he grows older is the American. Especially those Americans who live in the Middle West or even farther away, and whose attitude to many problems is often so different from that in New York and Washington. The British child assumes that all these people are cowboys. A number of Scottish schoolchildren of eleven were asked to write down all they knew about

the life and work of the cowboy. Their statements, based
primarily on the cinema but also on their reading, were after-
wards summarized as follows – and it seems unlikely that
television Westerns have since done much to modify their ideas:

> A cowboy is a man who looks very handsome. He always
> wears a belt with two guns in case of rustlers or wild animals.
> Every morning when he rises he bathes in a nearby stream. He
> is always jolly and when watching his cattle plays all the time on
> his guitar. He has a good voice and is a good cook. Cowboys go
> round the Red Indian tribes to see that they do not get up to mis-
> chief. Some cowboys drive the pony express. Some earn their
> living by robbing stage-coaches and stealing cattle. In the town,
> which is usually a far way off, there is one saloon and one barber.
> When the cowboys go into town they spend all their money in
> the saloon. The cowboy is different from every other man – he
> does not bother about churches and coat-tails. Most of them
> have no wives and live a carefree life.

Fifty pounds will not buy so very many books. Let us hope
that none of the money will be spent on stories which give
pictures of life abroad as false as that.

Strictly speaking, the cowboy story should now be shelved
with historical fiction. F. V. Morley's *War Paint* deals, to be
precise, with Indians and fur-traders on the North-West
Pacific coast in the early nineteenth century. Honoré Willsie
Morrow's *Splendid Journey* tells of Kit Carson and the Oregon
trail. 'Thousands of acres of it, to be had for the taking,' says a
character surveying the virgin territory before him. 'And if we
Americans don't take it, the British will.' That flash of national
feeling will not hurt the young British reader: it may prove
illuminating. The similar settings of Canada and Alaska will
always fascinate boys, and amid the mound of books which have
been written the buyer should try to find, dig out and examine
these titles which, though not in every case faultless, combine
good stories with a high degree of accuracy: Armstrong Sperry's
Wagons Westward, John Robb's *Sioux Arrow* and *Ten Guns for
Shelby*, Jack O'Brien's *Corporal Corey of the Royal Canadian*

Mounted, H. V. Coryell's *Klondike Gold*, and Muriel Denison's *Susannah of the Yukon* and *Susannah of the Mounties*. Books which give a less sensational side of North American life are two war-time evacuee stories, P. L. Travers's *I Go By Sea, I Go By Land* (United States) and Marjorie Sankey's *Stay for the Winter* (small Canadian town), as well as D. Gates's *Blue Willow*, set in the Californian cotton-fields, Emma Jacobs's *Trailer Trio* (Idaho) and Elizabeth Enright's *Thimble Summer*, a tale of Wisconsin farmers.

Looking quickly round the other countries popular with the adventure-story writer, we find that Herbert Best, himself a Colonial official, has written well of Nigeria. J. M. Scott, the explorer, has utilized his experiences in Greenland. East Africa is the scene of A. S. K. Davis's *A Farm in Cedar Valley*, and the Australian bush of M. I. Ross's *Greentree Downs*, which it is interesting to compare with Captain Johns's *Worrals Down Under*. Elizabeth Foreman Lewis's *Young Fu of the Upper Yangtze* should, with her other and with Pearl Buck's stories, do something to offset the impression left by Dr Fu Manchu. India can be represented by Dhan Gopal Mukerji's *Hari the Jungle Lad* and *Gay-Neck*, and John Budden's *Jungle John*; a more comprehensive picture – so comprehensive that it becomes a shade didactic at times – is given in *Tewari* by D. and H. Hogg, who cram in floods, earthquakes, communal riots over injured cows, Gandhi, the Depressed Classes, and most of the other things one ought to know about the country. Naomi Mitchison's more recent *Judy and Lakshmi* is a far better book about modern India, but is concerned with personal relationships rather than thrills, and is really a girl's book. Robert Gibbings covers the South Seas in *Coconut Island*. Most, if not all, of these authors write from first-hand experience and with a sense of responsibility. Yet none of their books has that hold on boys and girls which the 'Biggles' and 'Worrals' stories possess. 'How children's librarians long,' wrote one of them in a fierce attack upon Captain Johns and all his works, 'for the author who will write books the literary merit and technical quality of which will equal the zest found in Biggles.' It is a familiar cry. Sincerity, simplicity, enthusiasm: those were the three requisites demanded by G. J. H. Northcroft in *Writing for Children*. 'The boy wants two qualities in his books,' said Henry Dwight Sedgwick, 'enthusiasm and loyalty.' Enthusiasm, or zest, is the common factor. Until other adventure-story writers are prepared to let themselves go, they will never beat Biggles – or the comics. Once more the root of the matter lies deep. As was suggested in the opening chapter, when morals were discussed, too many of us have too little faith in anything, and without faith in something, however crude, false or obsolete, the adventure-story flags.

Authors like Henty and Ballantyne shared the dynamic of their period, more easily paralleled today in the Communist countries than in the West. Our own world is not deficient in robust adventures: the United Nations volunteers have built up their own body of sagas already, there are the roving television commentators who dodge along the bullet-sprayed boulevards where new sovereign states are being born, there are the idealists who challenge *apartheid* or segregation in the Deep South or any one of a dozen corrupt tyrannies to be found without straying beyond the limits of what we so ironically call 'the free world'. The adventure story, as always, lags behind contemporary reality. Even when the themes appear modern to us, they are already almost historical to the children. Ian Serraillier's *The Silver Sword* is about war-time Poland, Lawrence Durrell's *White Eagles Over Serbia* about secret service work in Yugoslavia, and Naomi Mitchison's *The Rib of the Green Umbrella* about the Italian Resistance. It is important that the children of the nineteen-sixties should read about the nineteen-forties – but they need to read about the nineteen-sixties too. Richard Church's *Dog Toby*, about frontier-tensions in Central Europe, remains all too topical, and J. M. Scott's *The Bright Eyes of Danger*, set in an imaginary People's Democracy on an East Mediterranean island, handles problems and situations still common enough. Here lies the advantage of using Ruritanian countries, and not always taking one's theme straight from the news bulletins. What we most need is an illumination, for the child, of the general problems facing the world – poverty, corruption, terrorism, exploitation – and of the adventure implicit in fighting against them. One Latin American republic, under a fictitious name, will serve for several – or one Arab oil state, one emergent African nation, or one Asian. Nor need the antagonist in the drama be always human, the conflict ideological. The annals of relief-work, the World Health Organization and other efforts, contain their own adventurous episodes, their own heroes, sometimes their own martyrs.

To many people, unfortunately, the future is attractive and interesting only in terms of technical achievement, and this bias is shared by writers of the adventure story who turn to science fiction as a popular and uncontroversial form. 'No boys' comic or magazine is complete without its space story,' says Mrs Fisher in *Intent Upon Reading*. 'No publisher's list is complete without at least one writer who knows how to get into a space-suit. But the really vital writers for children in this sphere are as scarce as inhabited planets.' Science fiction can be anything from an intelligent, informative stimulant to the imagination, a subtle criticism of things-as-they-are, a legitimate escape into fantasy – to the crudest melodrama (Mrs Fisher speaks of the 'brashly imperialistic flavour') in which the heroes have done little more than change sola topi for space-helmet. The wide range of quality is well illustrated by looking through a mixed dozen – say John Keir Cross's *Angry Planet* and *S.O.S. from Mars*, John Wyndham's *The Chrysalids*, Donald Suddaby's *Prisoners of Saturn*, Patrick Moore's *Captives of the Moon* and *Raiders of Mars*, Hugh Walters' *Blast Off at Woomera*, David Craigie's *Voyage of Luna I.*, W. E. Johns's *To Worlds Unknown*, one of Basil Dawson's *Dan Dare* stories and E. C. Eliott's numerous *Kemlo* books, and a Paul Berna (translated from the French), *Threshold of the Stars* or *Continent in the Sky*. Meriol Trevor's powerful *The Other Side of the Moon* does not quite fall into the conventional category of 'SF', and C. S. Lewis's *Out of the Silent Planet*, *Perelandra*, and *That Hideous Strength*, are no more children's books than are the romances of H. G. Wells and Edgar Rice Burroughs. But the age-barrier is nowhere more

G

meaningless than in this field, and Mrs Fisher frankly confesses: 'If boys over twelve really want to be stirred by exploration in space, by the feeling of alien worlds, I can only suggest that they give up children's books at once . . .'

Groom's early manual advised the young writer that 'the less one says about fighting the better, unless, of course, the story is for boys in their 'teens, and even then the less violence one spatters over one's MS. the more chance it will have of ultimately appearing in print.' Captain Johns, it will be remembered, was also opposed to unnecessary violence in fiction. It seems more than a little hard that, just when the popular writers were feeling most conscious of their moral responsibilities, they found themselves once more out of step with the pernickety educationists.

'I think,' James Hemming has said, 'children's literature should contain a certain amount of violence as a safety-valve for aggression.' A. S. Neill has expressed the view that a child needs to read, and sometimes to write, stories of violence. A Geneva report on *Children's Books and International Goodwill* declared in 1932 that 'the children of Iceland, though pacifist in tendency, delight in reading the war-like sagas of the twelfth and thirteenth centuries'. In this respect the young Icelanders are not unique.

Our children are not likely to go without the vitamin of violence in their literary diet, even though some writers decline to supply it. There is still plenty of stuff like this from *Bulldozer Brown*, by Steven Russell:

> He snatched up the battered chair and swung it round in a vicious semi-circle, so that it struck the heads of all three in quick succession.
>
> 'Yellow, eh?' shouted the boss. Wasting no time, he pulled out his revolver and shot the man down.

and this from Shalimar's *Sail Ho!*:

> Cedric swept three of them aside and punched another on the jaw.

What is necessary is to distinguish between the purposes for which violence is used, and the degree of approval which is implied by the writer. Is the violence used by the hero or the villain? If the former, is it justifiable? If the latter, does it go beyond reasonable bounds of supportable horror – is it sadistic? The nineteenth-century writers discriminated carefully. Today we have a tougher school of fiction, inspired in general by America and in particular by Ernest Hemingway, which favours no such romantic and chivalrous distinctions. 'You gotta be tough,' they say, in effect, to their readers. Queensberry rules, they might add if they knew what they were, don't work out in the real world. They have all too much evidence on their side. Their point of view was certainly adopted by the War Office in the training of Commandos. But have we come to such a pitch that we need to instil it in our juvenile fiction?

The common suggestion, even in the more old-fashioned and gentlemanly stories, is that a sock on the jaw is preferable to a reasoned argument or an appeal to proper authority. Peter Dawlish wrote in *The First Tripper*, an informative and well-written story of a cadet's first voyage:

> 'I'm not an officer now, I'm ashore. You can have it.' His fist caught Jarvis on the chin.

In *Warden of the Wilds*, by L. C. Douthwaite, we read:

> In the abandonment of a partner that desert-rat from the Prairie Provinces had been guilty of the unforgivable sin of the North, and Suddaby's urge was to live to meet the Irishman again. Then what happened to Slim O'Hagan would be his business and nobody else's.

This is a frequent theme in the 'robust' adventure-story. The virile character should take the law into his own hands. Any other form of redress is fit only for the 'sissy'.

We have said that for a boy a flesh-and-blood hero takes the place of an abstract ideal. If, therefore, the ideals we hold are of

Lance Cattermole

any importance, so is the type of hero we create to personify them.

'What do you find yourself looking for?' Anne Carroll Moore asked an American publisher. 'A real boy-hero kept in the foreground all the time,' he answered. 'The boy reader identifies himself with the hero, you know, and everything must feed through him.'

As a general tendency that is all very sound, but it seems a mistake to regard it (as some publishers and editors are beginning to do) as an immutable law. That would be to impose on adventure-fiction an intolerable limitation. The unthinking acceptance of the boy-hero as an absolute essential is contradicted by abundant experience. Where were the boys in *Sherlock Holmes*, *King Solomon's Mines*, *The Exploits of Brigadier Gerard*, *Greenmantle*, the literature of Robin Hood and Buffalo Bill – not to mention the contemporary Biggles?

The boy-hero came in with Ballantyne. As an ensign, a midshipman, and in a variety of other uniforms he fought his way through the seventy-odd stories of Henty. The ideal he personified was Christian manliness. 'Manliness,' records Harvey Darton, 'became in the long run rather wearisome.' The boy-hero 'often had no imagination or temperament of his own, and was only a type, conducting himself fearlessly, resourcefully and modestly in moments of great practical danger. . . . In England of course he was emphatically British, in the United States as emphatically American. The hero was the plain boy, who dislikes singularity, and eventually becomes a bore.'

Now the extraordinary thing is that the men who in real life have the kind of adventure described in fiction are anything but plain, and, so far from disliking singularity, not seldom arouse other people's dislike by their own excess of that quality. Think of Burton, searching for the Nile source, taking his life in his hands on the Mecca pilgrimage, translating the *Arabian Nights* in the bawdiest version we possess, and making a nuisance of himself in H. M. Consular Service. Think of the intellectual Ralegh, combining politics, chemistry, poetry, ship-design, theological speculation and a dozen other interests, with romantic quests for El Dorado. Think of Lawrence, who spent his school-holidays cycling from one castle to the next, and so was drawn on step by step, through archaeology, to leading the revolt in the desert, and back to that cottage in Dorset, with its five hundred books, and a strangely sympathetic relationship with Thomas Hardy, half a century his senior. And how many fiction-writers would dare to invent a boy-hero on these lines:

> He was not more serious at games. Football was cold and pointless. He did not want to score a goal any more than he wanted to be kicked on the shins. 'And,' he said, 'you get so cold rushing through the air like this.' The only possible way to get amusement out of such a sport was by shouting, 'Pass, pass!' until he got the ball and then kicking it into the dyke which ran beside the field. Cricket was a waste of pleasant weather. In the junior game, above which he never rose, he and Quentin Riley used to go in first. If Quentin got out before him, Gino would knock his own wicket down next ball; and then they would go off together to amuse themselves.

I quote from J. M. Scott's biography of Gino Watkins, who was to find Greenland even colder than football, but not 'pointless'.

It is the adventures of fiction that are often pointless. They are usually undertaken either for some selfish motive such as the quest for treasure, or for that abstract 'love of adventure' which one so seldom encounters in life. The real adventurer is impelled by many motives: geographical curiosity, a passion for archaeology or anthropology or botany or some other science, humanitarian or political ideals. The fictional hero is allowed none of these, least of all the last. The real adventurer has a heightened zest for life, and accepts danger not for its own sake but as unavoidable if he is to fulfil his purpose. The fictional hero is bored with civilized life, and lacks the imagination to find interests at home – he does not know, as any man with first-hand experience could tell him, that the acme of boredom is reached in the jungle or the desert, in the soldier's slit-trench or the fugitive's hide-out.

The fashionable hero after the war was the cheery, beefy ex-R.A.F. 'type'. Bulldozer Brown is a good example, 'very broad and thick-set, with a wide, square-cut face'. This is how he and his friend are introduced to the reader:

> London had begun to pall. Demobilized a few months, they had found cash getting rather low, too, and it had looked as if they would have to start in shortly on some wretchedly dull jobs. Somehow there did not seem much going in the job line – not of the kind that appealed to them, anyway, after over five years of the sort of thing that had gained them their pretty collection of ribbons. Civilian life didn't appear to offer much scope for the peculiar abilities of Squadron-Leader Brown and Flight-Lieutenant Chubb.

We feel we know them already. We have met them in Service messes. We have seen their optimistic advertisements in the Personal columns, mentioning no qualifications more specialized than the ability to drive a car and the willingness to 'go anywhere, do anything'. What happens to them in real life? They seldom get any nearer to adventure than some plantation job in one of those dwindling areas where a white skin still compensates for all other shortcomings. Rather more is required of the man who is to investigate the Greenland ice-cap, dig up a lost city in the Yucatán jungle, or even carry on the routine of colonial administration in the Solomons.

Perhaps this examination of the hero-type throws a little light on why so many good writers are unable to produce convincing and popular adventure-stories. Heroes are out of fashion in sensitive intellectual circles. The preoccupation of the modern novelist has for a long time been the weakness, rather than the strength, of human nature. We have seen the vogue for the 'debunking' biography. Most of all do we distrust any encouragement of that 'leader-principle', which is implicit in the Biggles stories. What did their fourteen-year-old admirer comment on? 'A born leader of men. . . . The supporting characters back him up in everything he does and do not argue too much. Their chief virtue is that they hero-worship. . . .'

Yet Colin Wilson was right when he wrote in *The Age of Defeat*: 'For the schoolboy, the future may be unknown, but one thing is certain: it is full of interesting possibilities. All adults are failures (except, perhaps, one's favourite film-stars). They have sold out too cheaply, exchanged their endless possibilities for a few boring actualities. . . . It is true that the schoolboy's demand for these qualities in his heroes comes from a lack of acquaintance with the real world. But the schoolboy has his own viewpoint: he feels that the adult acceptance of an unheroic world may spring from too much contact with the realities of that world – from a premature defeatism.' And William Faulkner was right, too, when he said, in his speech accepting the Nobel Prize for Literature in 1950, that it was the writer's privilege 'to help man endure by lifting his heart, by reminding him of the courage and honour and hope and pride and compassion and pity and sacrifice which have been the glory of his past.'

Make no mistake, our boys will have their heroes. They will not thrill to the long-drawn-out deliberations of a committee. But democracy and humanism have had their share of heroes (I use 'humanism' in its original, not atheistic, sense) and there is no reason why boys should not learn to love both them and, unconsciously, the ideals which they personify.

CHAPTER EIGHT

Cloak and Sword

T HOUGH the details of Scott's novels are not always correct they give one a very good idea of the period and though they are rather painful to read they always give benefit.

Thus, with tolerance unusual in a child, wrote Gillian Hansard in her *Old Books for the New Young*.

Many children will not read historical stories. It seems a matter of prejudice, rather than reasoned dislike. Often I have asked a school audience how many of them will put a book down without further examination, as soon as they see it is historical. Always there are a number of hands raised. Even more would go up if the children were not conscious that the speaker was himself a writer of such stories.

Yet, say some librarians, once get a child on to historical stories, and the battle is won – he comes back for more and more. The popularity of historical films is well-known. There is no prejudice against them, because they carry no lingering flavour of school, and make no extra mental demands, whereas an historical novel almost invariably uses a richer vocabulary than its modern counterpart and can hardly avoid an element of description.

The film too, and the television play, will use easy modern dialogue – sometimes gratingly banal, like the courtier's remark in a film-script about the Field of the Cloth of Gold, 'I do hate parties, don't you?' But it is easy; whereas the children's historical novel plodded on for several generations weighted down with unnecessary trappings inherited from Scott and Ainsworth. Books like Gertrude Hollis's *Spurs and Bride* were still on the shelves a few years ago, and may be now. This conscientious author, not content with footnotes, interjected explanations into the midst of the narrative:

> 'Yonder sight is enough to make a man eschew lance and sword for ever, and take to hot-cockles and cherry pit' (popular games), exclaimed the Earl of Pembroke adding an oath which the sacred character of the building did not in the least restrain.

Even with the parenthesis there must have been many a juvenile eye, hastily skipping along, which has read 'chew' for 'eschew' and transmitted to the brain a muddled image of some fantastic demonstration of sword-swallowing, with oysters and cherry-pie to follow. In more recent books by much better writers we find remarks such as 'I joy me' and 'Wot you what?' (D. M. Stuart) and – making the worst of both worlds – Carola Oman's 'I am not in a great hurry, if you truly desire aught, but I think I ought to be turning home now.'

It is only now, forty years after Naomi Mitchison so brilliantly pointed the way in *The Conquered*, that natural, modern but not anachronistic dialogue has finally won the day against the varlet-and-halidom type of language. Naomi Mitchison was, in that respect, my own inspiration when I began writing my first children's book in 1933, for I felt that archaic dialogue had strangled the life out of the historical story. 1934 saw the publication not only of my own little *Bows Against the Barons* and *Comrades for the Charter* but of an important and influential adult novel, Robert Graves's *I Claudius*, which was to accelerate the movement towards natural living speech which Mrs Mitchison had begun.

'Accelerate' is an almost ironical word. It was a slow process, bitterly resisted in some quarters. Today it seems self-evident that, if the reader accepts the convention of Arabs, Eskimos and even Martians conversing in modern English, Robin Hood and Friar Tuck should be permitted to do the same. After all, if we were to set down their actual thirteenth-century speech, it would be almost as unintelligible as Arabic, not only to boys but to the average adult. But there was never any suggestion that the Sherwood outlaws should use an authentic medieval diction, any more than that Claudius should tell his story in Latin. What was expected was a bogus sort of Wardour Street jargon which was supposed to 'convey period atmosphere', but which some of us would have said, more simply, stank. It is an old argument, over now. It would be difficult to find, among recent publications, a 'quotha!' or a 'Ha, we are beset!' The revolution in diction has probably contributed more than any other single factor to overcoming children's prejudice against the historical tale.

It is only one factor. Better characterization, livelier action, less hackneyed subjects, more vivid backgrounds, a poetic power to evoke something that really *is* 'atmosphere' and not the reek of moth-balls – all these have combined to produce an astonishingly rich florescence of this genre. Margaret Meek, in her first contribution to the Bodley Head monographs, is kind enough to suggest that the new era opened with *Cue for Treason* in 1940. 'Now,' she continues, 'the library shelves are crowded with historical tales, and authors of distinction, Rosemary Sutcliff, Cynthia Harnett, Rhoda Power, Ronald Welch, Henry Treece, Carola Oman and others, have found in this kind the task most suited to their talents and interests.' The process of improvement seems to me to have been cumulative. The amount of first-rate historical fiction published since this survey was originally written has gone far to transform the situation I criticized then.

Going on to speak of my 'stringent demands about accuracy', Miss Meek says that 'we can now recommend novels in history lessons with safety because every reputable writer takes this for granted'. There has been, I believe, an increasing respect for accuracy, not only among the authors but among the teachers, some of whom rather surprised me (in 1948) by their casual attitude. One said that accuracy was unimportant, provided that the book stirred the imagination. The elder Dumas would have emphasized that proviso. As he remarked, with French directness: 'One can violate History only if one has a child by her.' The inaccuracies in Dumas, Scott and the other

romantic giants of that era are readily forgiven, because of what
their broad effects achieved in rousing people to an interest in
the past. Indeed, even the most blatant cloak-and-sword
nonsense can be defended – it may have been the story which
first stirred some child's imagination at a critical moment in his
development, and led him on to better things. Let us grant this.
But let us not conclude that accuracy is without value. True,
as another teacher told me, 'it does not necessarily make a good
tale'. Does inaccuracy? Is it really essential to distort the truth
in order to produce an exciting plot?

To do so seems a confession of deficiency, since the more truly
imaginative an author is, the more colour and drama he can
reveal in things-as-they-were. Years ago there was a film called
The Charge of the Light Brigade. The scenario department felt
there was insufficient drama in the bald facts of that magnificent
but misguided manœuvre. They therefore 'built it up' by
starting the story some years back in India, where one of the
cavalry regiments concerned developed a feud with a certain
treacherous rajah. The Crimean War broke out; the rajah,
having found India too hot for him, had sought a change of
temperature in the obvious country – and we saw him at the
Battle of Balaklava, riding with the Russians as a sort of unofficial
foreign observer. The regiment saw him too. He was sneering
at them from a position behind the Russian guns. So they
charged, only incidentally for the guns. It was a very good
charge, and a good example of what can happen when you once
accept the suggestion that truth and entertainment are somehow
incompatible. Those who have subsequently read Mrs Cecil
Woodham-Smith's *The Reason Why* are not likely to accept it.

When I was writing *Trumpets in the West* in the middle of
India, with scarcely any reference-books, I discovered just in
time that the stage-coaches in 1686 carried no outside passengers.
It meant rewriting a complete chapter. Probably no child would
ever have noticed the mistake, and perhaps no History teacher
would have minded. But why *not* have it right? Or was it just
that some years of Service life had produced in me an intolerant
reaction against all who said: 'O.K., boy, if you can get away

with it!' Similarly, a whole chapter of *Thunder of Valmy* had to be rewritten when I discovered by chance that a certain morning at Versailles in May, 1789, had been grey and drizzly, not sunny as I had first pictured it. What does it matter, a pedantic detail like that? Just as much, or as little, as the workmanship which old-time sculptors and carvers put into figures so far from the ground that no human eye would ever appreciate it.

Of course, if the stone-carver breaks his neck, it emphatically isn't worth while. And if too much pedantic research breaks the spirit of a story, that isn't worth while either. That is why the teachers are broadly correct in what they say. They have seen far more historical stories deadened by ill-digested facts than distorted by falsehood. Conscientiousness is the tradition of the historical writer. George Eliot tore up the first draft of *Romola* because she found so many historical errors in it, and the final version 'changed her from a young woman to an old'. Charles Reade spent eighteen months on research for *The Cloister and the Hearth*; the same seriousness, applied to the writing of his South Seas novel, *Foul Play*, led him to have his walls and ceilings painted a vivid tropical blue. Few writers would take the quest for local colour as far as that. *Ivanhoe* would scarcely have been improved if Scott had worn a suit of armour while writing it. Fortunately the writer does not need to go to such heroic lengths. Today, equipped with a modest row of books on costume and other aspects of social history, and with the whole resources of the library service available to provide more specialized data, he should not find it difficult to maintain a reasonable standard of accuracy. Lapses still unaccountably occur. Thus, in *The Golden Cloak*, published in 1963, a story of Britain at the time of Julius Caesar by Paul Capon, we read of 'knights', 'jousting', and 'dungeons', of a ship's 'wardroom' and of a single herald blowing a 'fanfare', which one would have thought was not only an anachronism but a physical impossibility. Mr Capon's earlier story about Knossos, *The Kingdom of the Bulls*, was given the accolade of the *Time Literary Supplement* as being 'full of care and enthusiasm for the practical details of life'. But then authors, from Homer's time onwards, have been known to nod occasionally, and it is possible that critics do the same. The glaring mistake is certainly much rarer than it used to be.

The trouble is rather that too many historical writers have been even more in love with history than with writing. They are so fascinated by their discoveries (how well I know the danger!) that they are tempted to put them all in. So, as their knowledge increases, the story gets bogged down in detail. They describe and explain where they should be content to indicate. There is a good deal to be said for writing historical fiction in the depths of the Indian jungle. . . . But the more courageous way is to face your reference-books squarely across the table, and convince yourself that you, not they, are going to write the story.

G. M. Trevelyan defined the good historical novelist in these words: 'If he is to be anything more than a boiler of the pot, he requires two qualities: an historical mind, apt to study the records of a period, and a power of creative imagination able to reproduce the perceptions so acquired in a picture that has all the colours of life.' Nobody with an historical mind will ever excuse avoidable inaccuracy.

If books of this kind depart from truth it is not usually in trivial matters of dates or anachronisms of costume, but in the false general impression which they leave in the young reader's memory. Take, for example, the French Revolution. The modern teacher presumably presents this event in the class-room in a balanced and objective way, with due regard to its causes and its consequences in Europe. Without minimizing the horrors of the Reign of Terror, he no doubt points out that this was merely a brief episode in a long, necessary and on the whole progressive historical movement. He wishes the period to come alive for the class, and he racks his brains for stories which he can read aloud or recommend. A lecturer in Education once asked me to suggest fiction he could include in a leaflet for student-teachers, for he could think of nothing but *A Tale of Two Cities* and *The Scarlet Pimpernel*.

Both these adult novels (and the host of juvenile imitations they have produced) are uncompromisingly counter-Revolutionary in tone. Dickens was perhaps too near the events in time, too much influenced by the lingering prejudices of the Napoleonic period, to apply the same radical approach to French problems as he brought to bear on English. It is said that when he consulted Carlyle on the period, Carlyle sent round a cart-load of books. It is well that Dickens did not read them all, but a pity perhaps that he did not read some. I could think of only one adult novel, Belloc's *The Girondin*, which gave anything like the opposite point of view.

My own boyhood impressions of the French Revolution were all gained from a story by A. S. Walkey, *In the Reign of Terror*, all about a debonair Englishman, 'Jack-o'-Lantern', who spirited French aristocrats away to safety from the very shadow of the guillotine. These impressions (which somehow never got modified by any class-room teaching) were confirmed when, in my middle-teens, I saw Martin Harvey in *The Only Way*. Only in later years did I discover that there had been debonair Frenchmen like Lafayette, rich and human (if rough and ready) characters like Danton, and drama in the guns of Valmy, the music of the Marseillaise. . . . Walkey wrote quite well. He made no historical howlers. It was just that he gave only one small, not very significant fragment of the truth. Unfortunately all the other stories give exactly the same bit.

Dorothea Moore's *In the Reign of the Red Cap* is a fair example. It is written with an evident knowledge of the period. Apart from a few creaking coincidences, it is a good little story. But the aristocratic bias is there from the title page almost to the last epithet. The hero has a 'pale, proud, handsome young face and a slender, graceful figure in torn grey velvet and satin'. The 'mob' are a 'savage crew'. Epithets applied to them include "bloated", "unkempt" and "greasy" – one even wears a 'greasy hat'. They show their 'stained teeth' in a 'wolfish grin', and the sounds which issue vary from 'drunken oaths' to 'horrid howls'. When their nefarious business calls for quieter behaviour they 'skulk'. Ronald Welch's *Escape from France*, a more recent and much better written story, keeps none the less to the old

Pimpernel tradition, dealing as it does with an aristocratic Cambridge undergraduate who rescues a French relative from the Revolution.

One children's novel, Marjorie Bowen's *Strangers to Freedom*, consciously attempts a fairer picture. In an eight-page foreword (which, combined with a rather slowly starting plot, may deter many children from an otherwise enjoyable book), she says: 'There are more stories than anyone can count dealing with these most exciting times, but most of them deal in very broad effects; the so-called "revolutionaries" are always villains and the "aristocrats" heroes and heroines, rescued from "the rabble" by bold Englishmen or their own courage. Such tales, however interesting as adventure stories, are usually written by people who know nothing about history, with the result that if we read nothing but fiction on this great epoch of modern history, we shall have a very false impression.'

After those admirable sentiments it seems a pity that Miss Bowen still chose, herself, to write from the aristocratic side, although with much greater objectivity. So too, when she turned to another much-favoured theme, she produced *The Trumpet and the Swan*, 'a tale of the Civil War in England and a boy's attempt to bring aid to King Charles'. The fiction-writer's Cavalier sympathies are almost invariable. To explain this away as due to the fascination of lost causes and the British feeling for the under-dog is muddled thinking. The Armada and many other events popular in fiction were anything but lost causes from the English viewpoint – and there have been plenty of picturesque enough under-dogs, like the English peasant in 1381, the French in 1789, and the Spanish* in 1936, who still await a fairer share of sympathetic treatment. It is true that L. A. G. Strong gives in *King Richard's Land* an account of the Peasants' Revolt which is a vast improvement on Henty's *March on London*, where Wat Tyler is characteristically described as 'an insolent varlet' leading our old friends, 'the mob'. But

---

* I have met only one juvenile story dealing with the Spanish Civil War, Westerman's *Under Fire in Spain*. The hero was an English boy serving with General Franco.

even Strong picked his boy-heroes from the upper class, and they are heirs to great feudal estates. Carola Oman (*Ferry the Fearless*), and Magdalen King-Hall (*Jehan of the Ready Fists*) are two more very able writers on the medieval scene – but both, it seems, feel more at home behind castle walls. The bias, however, is never more marked than it is in the Civil War stories. *True to the King, The King's Namesake, For Rupert and the King, The Royalist Brothers* . . . they used to flood from the presses every season. The flow has dwindled, but many of these old books are still on the shelves, with little but Rosemary Sutcliff's *Simon* to suggest that there was another point of view.

We come back to the same question which was discussed in the previous chapter: what heroes should we be holding up to our children? The historical story is, after all, only an adventure story with certain added special characteristics. There is no logical reason why mystery, humour, school-life and the other main themes should not be presented in an historical guise, but somehow they never are. There is a convention that life was more adventurous and exciting in 'the olden days'; it is almost certainly untrue for the vast majority of the population, but it dies hard. So we come back to our heroes.

The Cavalier and the Jacobite, the sea-dog and the French aristocrat, might well be turned out to grass for a while. So might the knight in shining armour. They have been ridden almost to death. They figure not only in a host of bad books but in a quite adequate list of good ones. Now we need some new heroes. There is no field of endeavour without them, no historically significant theme which cannot be dramatized.

It is now possible to build up a richly varied library of historical fiction representing (though sometimes admittedly misrepresenting) almost every period from the cavemen onwards. For what we used to call, with convenient imprecision, 'the Ancient Britons', we have Rosemary Sutcliff's *Warrior Scarlet*, Henry Treece's *Men of the Hills*, Joyce Reason's *Bran the Bronze-Smith* and *Swords of Iron*, and Dorothy Severn's *Kerin the Watcher*. Roman Britain and its chaotic aftermath are equally well covered, notably by Miss Sutcliff and Mr Treece, both of whom excel in evoking the atmosphere of early and primitive times. We could continue the book-list down the centuries, and it is encouraging to see how themes which a generation ago would have been ignored or would have received only the most hackneyed treatment are handled in several highly individual ways by as many skilful different hands. Take for instance the Norsemen. The dependable Miss Sutcliff and Mr Treece are there, the former with *The Shield Ring*, set in Cumberland, and the latter with *Viking's Dawn, Viking's Sunset*, and *The Road to Miklagard*. But there is another good trilogy by Dr Alan Boucher, who brings from his studies at the University of Reykjavik the specialist equipment of a scholar – as well as a flair for story-telling which helps him to impart a true saga-like flavour to *The Wineland Venture* and the books which precede it. Here his young Icelandic hero fares beyond even Greenland to the island we now call Newfoundland. Naomi Mitchison starts from her own Scotland and for her *The Land the Ravens Found* is Iceland. Marion Campbell, an expert in Scottish archaeology, shows in *Lances and Longships* how as late as the thirteenth century the Scotsmen of the Western Isles were more involved with Norwegian enemies than English. And in yet another good story, Eileen O'Faolain's *High Sang the Sword*, we can discover how these ubiquitous Norsemen fared against Brian Boru in eleventh-century Ireland. When we survey a pile of volumes like these, all variations on a single historical theme, none falling below a quite considerable standard of quality, we can begin to realize the remarkable advance of children's literature in this field during the past quarter of a century, and even more during the last decade.

There is still infinite scope – still much of the old need to correct the traditional bias in favour of the nobly-born hero and the fighter rather than the man of peace – but even here there is much improvement. Cynthia Harnett is pre-eminent in this field, with her London merchants in *Ring Out Bow Bells*, the Cotswold wool-trade in *The Wool-Pack*, and Caxton's printing works in *The Load of Unicorn*. Other books which have attempted, with varying success, to find inspiration in the workaday world are Henry Garnett's *Rough Water Brown* and *Secret of the Rocks* (about the old-time river traffic on the Severn), Agnes Ashton's *Water for London* (Middleton's New River project of 1609), A. Stephen Tring's *Young Master Carver* (craftsmanship in the reign of Edward III), L. A. G. Strong's *Mr Sheridan's Umbrella* (umbrella-factory in Regency Brighton), and Laurence Meynell's *Bridge Under the Water* (Brunel's building of the Thames Tunnel). The entertainment business has always been popular with the historical story-teller: we have Rosemary Sutcliff's *Brother Dusty-Feet*, John Bennett's *Master Skylark*, and Frederick Grice's *Aidan and the Strollers* (Edmund Kean period), with E. J. Gray's *Adam of the Road* taking us back to the era of the medieval minstrel, while, for a change, *His Majesty's Players* by C. M. Edmondston and M. L. F. Hyde carries the 'Elizabethan' theatre on to its last days under Charles I.

Rockbottom working-class life is shown in Magdalen King-Hall's *Sturdy Rogue*, Ivy Bolton's *Son of the Land* (Wat Tyler again), and Jack Lindsay's *Runaway* (Spartacus revolt), this last written nearly thirty years ago by a powerful and prolific writer who is both a classical scholar and a Marxist, and a slave is also the central figure of Miss Sutcliff's *Outcast*. It is worth noting, incidentally, that the hero of her *Knight's Fee* starts with the humble status of kennel-boy, and that in *The Noble Hawks* by Ursula Moray Williams a nice question of class-inequality is touched upon, since Dickon, the yeoman's son, is allowed only a goshawk, a bird as low in the social scale of falcons as the boy himself in the feudal community.

CHAPTER NINE

Midnight in the Dorm

FOR Sale: Large desirable residence on remote part Cornish coast; smugglers' caves, secret passage, treacherous tides, suitable school or institution . . .
Penblethering Priory: qualified staff, incl. resident enemy agent. Inspected by Min. of Edn. and C.I.D. Farm produce, gravel subsoil . . .

If advertisements like these are rare in our newspapers it is possibly because school stories bear little relation to reality. 'We have looked through several schoolgirls' annuals,' the principals of a London school once wrote to me, 'and find they give a very false view of school life. The fourth form seem to run the school – the headmistress is generally a dignified but distant figure-head, and the assistant mistresses either young, very girlish and so popular, or middle-aged caricatures. In one a party of girls were allowed to go for a picnic some miles from the school without any mistress. Among them was a "Ruritanian" princess with a gang of international crooks after her. She had been sent to the school for safety and was naturally kidnapped on the picnic.' Never mind. She will be seen again – and again, oh, so often – as we continue our researches into this class of children's fiction.

'The school story,' wrote George Orwell in *Inside the Whale*, 'is a thing peculiar to England. So far as I know there are extremely few school stories in foreign languages.' The boy's school story is as old as the present Public School system, for *Tom Brown*, published in 1856, was the direct and rapid result of Arnold's epoch-making headmastership. *Eric* followed only two years later. Curiously enough, the author who really set the pattern of the school story was not himself, save in a technical sense, a Public School man. Talbot Baines Reed went to a London day school, and knew the life of St Dominic's and Fellsgarth only at second hand. That did not matter. In conjunction with the *Boy's Own Paper*, then a young and vigorous force in juvenile fiction, he created a literary convention acceptable even to many boys at boarding-school and entirely satisfactory to the much wider public excluded from what Orwell called 'that mystic world of quadrangles and house colours'.

Reed was born six years before *Eric*: he died six years before *Stalky and Co*. – Kipling's 'mucky little sadists', as Wells called them in his *Autobiography* – burst upon the world in 1899. The influence of Stalky was immeasurable. It is from this book, as Orwell convincingly argued, that the school stories in such boys' weeklies as the *Gem* and the *Magnet* derived. There has been no comparable infusion of new life in the fifty years that have passed since then. Vachell's *The Hill*, in 1905, was in the *Eric* tradition. The series of frank, autobiographical stories which began not with Waugh's *The Loom of Youth*, but with Lunn's *The Harrovians* a few years before, and which reached such a pitch by 1930 that an Old Boys' Society felt slighted until it was given the excuse to expel at least one budding young novelist from its membership, can scarcely be included with ordinary school stories. They can, however, be very fine reading for the boy who is well into adolescence. I remember how I was moved by Beverley Nichols' first precocious novel, *Prelude*. Here, I realized with surprise, relief and the joy of recognition, are characters who feel and think as I do. The first book which does that for a boy or girl is not a milestone but a bridge, carrying them over from the love of romance to the appreciation of reality. From *Prelude* I went on to Compton Mackenzie's *Sinister Street*.

The girls' school story, for obvious historical reasons, lagged many years behind. Its Talbot Baines Reed was Angela Brazil, who died as recently as 1947. Long before then two other prolific writers were following in her footsteps, Elsie J. Oxenham, with her numerous *Abbey* stories from 1920 onwards, and E. Brent Dyer, whose first *Chalet School* story appeared in

1925. After these series we come to the school stories of Enid
Blyton.

The low level of writing in this field is not hard to understand
if we turn to Arthur Groom's manual and read his advice to
the aspirant in 1929: 'Before commencing one's first school
story, one should obtain either from a young relation or friend
. . . some idea of the prevailing conditions in our large public
schools – for it is of these that one should principally write.'
Let me interrupt to ask, why? And to suggest that the author
who really wrote of 'prevailing conditions' would give a
picture so different from that of the conventional story that it
would be unrecognizable.

'With regard to ideas,' Arthur Groom continued, 'the best
method of obtaining them is to put into words those beautiful
day-dreams of one's youth. To bring off that marvellous catch;
to rescue the headmaster's little daughter from the mill-stream . . .
to stumble across the cache of silver articles stolen from the
home of the school Governor; to win the "Mile" with one's
arm hanging at one's side after the school bully has fouled one
on the bend; to struggle against the swift current in the river
with the youngest girl in the school clinging round one's neck,
and to save one's favourite mistress from financial disaster.'
It is advisable to use the last idea only in girls' stories. 'Make
the characters,' he concluded, 'live the lives of ordinary, healthy
human boys and girls.'

One new tendency is discernible over those years – the
increasing reliance on crime, ranging from petty local burglary
to large-scale smuggling and foreign espionage. In the old days
this was left to the cheap weeklies, and established authors felt
there was sufficient drama inherent in school life, with its dormitory feeds, broken bounds and vital sporting fixtures,
without secret passages and hooded figures. These secret
passages, like Mr Groom's 'cache of silver articles' and other
variants of the treasure theme, may be symbols of dark psychological meaning, but, as the bishop remarked in the temple of
Siva, even a symbol can be over-stressed. I recall receiving three

school stories for review from a firm usually described as 'educational publishers'. Each was by a different author, but each contained a secret passage and a hidden hoard.

Absurd and repetitive plots; stereotyped characterization; latent (and sometimes blatant) snobbery; occasionally what Orwell termed 'a perfectly deliberate incitement to wealth-fantasy'; and a laboured facetiousness of style . . . these have been the salient qualities in the majority of school stories. 'An iceberg would have boiled a kettle of water quicker than their temperatures at that moment' and 'A coin of the realm exchanged ownership' are fair samples of style. Contrast with them the colloquial first-hand narrative of A. Stephen Tring's *The Old Gang*, a good story about Grammar School day-boys which broke new ground in 1947. It had no literary quality in the conventional sense, but it spoke with the authentic voice of a boy:

> Mums came up with them and said . . . 'Joe, I rely on you as head of your group or whatever you call it—'
> 'Gang, Mums,' I said, 'gang, for heaven's sake.'
> And again:
> 'She wasn't wearing the black and red affair that she had on up at the Grammar, but a tweed business which was sort of greeny yellowy mixed and looked awfully smart.'

How is this for a new version of that recurrent scene, the car smash:

> I don't know if you have ever been in a car smash; I never had before this one and now I can quite understand anybody who is involved and who is asked to give evidence afterwards about what happened not being the slightest use.
> The truth is you just don't know. I was in that Rover when it overturned, and as far as I know I was not knocked on the head or anything like that which might have made me unconscious for a moment, but it is literal truth that the first thing I remember

about it, after seeing the hedge coming in as it seemed through the windows, was standing on the road trying to get one of my shoes on.

How clumsy? Yes, but how intensely alive. With boys the two qualities are apt to go together. We do not want children's literature swamped with the purely colloquial, spattered with 'sort of' and 'like' for 'as', but it would be better than 'coin of

the realm' instead of 'sixpence'. 'If the moribund boy's story is to recover its vitality,' I wrote in 1948, 'a transfusion of Stephen Tring is our best hope. The more imaginative vocabulary must follow when the patient is strong enough to digest it.' As we shall see in a moment, a good deal has happened since then.

Not everyone agrees that there is harm in the implicit

snobbery of the average school story. The chairman of a Parents' Guild wrote that it was 'like water off a duck's back', and the English mistress of a High School said that as these stories 'present so obviously unreal a picture, the question of promoting snobbery does not arise'. It might be worth looking at a typical story, Judith Grey's *Duchess in Disguise*.

Olive's father having died, she has spent the last few terms very unhappily at the boarding-school kept by her mother's old friend, who has kindly taken her on reduced terms. The other girls, knowing this, but apparently not knowing that there is someone 'on reduced terms' in every private school (cynics might say, every child), have christened her Charity Girl. When the story opens, her mother's rich uncle Jeremiah has considerately died and restored the family fortunes, so that Olive is able to inform her school-mates on the last day of term: 'We're richer now than any six of you put together. Next term I shall go to a really first-class school. Whatever it costs, Mother can afford it now. That's all. Will you please go away, every one of you? This is my room for an hour yet and I want to be alone.' Whereupon her tormentors, somewhat improbably, 'melt away as silently as possible, quiet and wondering'.

Olive's mother has a 'great respect for position and title'. The kindness of her old friend, the headmistress, is repaid (but not apparently the balance of the reduced terms) by Olive's immediate transfer to Sedley Manor, where 'Lord Arncliffe had a girl and the twin daughters of a very eminent painter were also among the pupils'. What could her old friend's 'cheap and struggling' school (though not so cheap that reduced terms had not been welcome) offer to compete with attractions such as these? Mrs Hartley is 'an aristocrat to her finger-tips'. Olive discards the 'rags' which had been good enough for her old school, and lays in a stock of glamorous undies and sports-wear worthy of a newly contracted film-star.

Her new school-mates are unimpressed. Luckily there has been a news-item mentioning that a foreign Grand Duchess has been sent as a pupil, incognita, to an unspecified but exclusive English school. Desperate for popularity, Olive drops a few skilful hints that she is the 'duchess in disguise', whereupon, being daughters of 'the very best people', the rest of the school fall at her feet.

Alas for Olive! The real duchess is there – she is Marie, the imperious class-mate, whose friendship Olive (with her mother's nose for blue blood) desires more ardently than anyone else's. Marie denounces her imposture. Mrs Hartley is summoned and, with a mother's infallible instinct, lays her finger on Olive's fault – she is too fond of fairy-tales. 'I shall take your Hans Andersen and *Arabian Nights* back home with me and you will please read no more fairy books this term.' Olive has to make abject confession to the assembled school, is gated and ostracized for the rest of the term, but on the last day Marie forgives her. 'The Grand Duchess laughed deliciously . . . These two who had been estranged were laughing and crying with their arms round each other.' The moral is made clear: 'Popularity has to be earned, not cheated for.' It is all right to go hysterical over a title, but you must not pretend to one which isn't yours. After all, if we can't trust the label, how can we choose our friends? This book was published in 1943, when there was some talk about democracy.

'One must never write about drink,' wrote Mr Groom long ago, 'or love in its passionate form.' Except possibly, he might have added, in terms of no less passionate disapproval. It is seldom that alcohol or sex is even indirectly referred to in school stories. Only once in a while does one encounter a moral tale of the good old stamp, like Grace Pettman's *The Queensgate Mystery*. The usual ingredients are there – the girls' school on the cliffs, secret passage, smugglers and a heroine with an aura of mystery. But there is something more. On the first night at her new school Joan is horrified to find another girl in the dormitory reading something so vaguely indicated that the average young reader (at least in pre-Penguin-Chatterley days) was probably completely mystified by all the fuss. The one who showed me the story, which had been given her as a birth-day present, certainly was, and consequently curious.

'I've been on the continent a lot where such – such books are openly read, and openly discussed . . . Oh, Kath – Madge, you are old enough to know that you are touching pitch. Pitch cannot be touched without defiling the soul . . . Why, that book is not allowed to be printed or published in England at all . . .'

Madge, her voice full of suppressed passion, hissed the word. 'Sneak! Spy! You mean to tell?'

Joan makes no immediate decision, but lies in bed meditating after Lights Out.

'My first night at Queensgate Castle, and what a night,' groaned Joan. 'Oh, Lord, I did so want to witness for Thee here, and yet not be obliged to do anything that the other girls would condemn as mean. But now I'm fairly up against it. What am I to do?'

She is spared the decision. Matron picks up a loose page of the offending volume which has blown under one of the beds, and carries it to the headmistress. It is evidently hot stuff, for the headmistress 'drops it quickly as if it scorched her fingers'. A dormitory search reveals the rest of the book, and, horror upon horror, 'a couple of French novels, one a translation, the other in the original'. Some heads might derive compensating pleasure from this last evidence of linguistic ability, but not so Miss Cambridge. She knows the truth of that dark philosophical remark dropped by the author on page 31: 'Cause and effect, and effect and cause, lead to all sorts of things . . .'

The subsequent discovery of the secret passage is especially gratifying to Miss Cambridge, because it is being used for the smuggling of liquor.

Her nostrils were assailed by a pungent odour – not of night-scented stock or evening primrose, but the smell of something she hated like poison – for she knew that to many a man and woman it was veritable poison, a curse indeed.

In laboratory work and in such Social Service as had come her way, Miss Cambridge had become more or less familiar with the unmistakable reek of alcohol. Brandy? Gin? What was it? She hated the reek of them all.

This book was published in 1933 and had been reprinted four times up to 1947. Doubtless it is still on many a library shelf.

The Queensgate Mystery may not be typical of recent school stories, but it is probably true to say that the moral – more subtly presented – survives more vigorously and consciously in this type of book than anywhere else. 'Children's writers have definite responsibilities towards their young public,' Enid Blyton told me. 'For this reason they should be certain always that their stories have sound morals – children *like* them. Right should always be right, and wrong should be wrong, the hero should be rewarded, the villain punished.' Most really competent observers seem agreed that children like morals if they are artistically woven into the fabric of the story, and not pinned on. It is only the adult who fights shy of them. The important thing is that the moral should be concerned with the problems of the child's own life, or at least within its normal range of observation. No one, incidentally, should be misled by title of Miss Blyton's book, *Five get into Trouble*.

As to the religious question, there will be legitimate difference of opinion: those who consider that religious belief is the basis of character-building from the earliest years, not something to be left 'till the child is old enough to decide for itself', will reasonably demand that it should be reflected in fiction. The agnostic may concede the point, on condition that the belief is fairly presented (preferably through the characters rather than through the author) and that occasionally alternative views may be indicated. We do not want either school stories or any other stories to become theological debating-grounds, but if religion *is* to be mentioned as a moral influence it is only fair to combat the prejudiced view that Christianity alone helps people to lead decent lives. The faith of the Jew, the Muslim, the Hindu and the Buddhist must be taken into account, and the possibility that some intelligent and admirable people behave themselves quite well without being aware of any supernatural support whatever. So many adults refuse to believe the evidence of their own eyes on this last point that it might be well if an occasional story were presented to children before their prejudices became hopelessly ingrown. What we do *not* want is the encouragement of juvenile preachers, immature moralists and adolescent ascetics. There is enough turgid religious emotion at that age without the writer to whip it up.

For an example of Miss Blyton's school fiction at its best, take *The Naughtiest Girl in the School*. The theme is the first term of a spoilt little girl at a progressive co-educational boarding-school – a most unusual setting,* at the time, for juvenile fiction is conspicuously insensible to the changes of the last few decades. Desmond Coke, himself a notable writer of school stories, remarked in his preface to *The Worm* in 1927: 'Education is, in these days, so vital that every serious school story must of necessity have theories below it: to underline them is bad art.' Thomas Hughes would have agreed with the first part if not the second. Yet, though Arnold's revolution at Rugby quickly produced the classic *Tom Brown*, the other outstanding changes in education during the past hundred years find no notable reflection in stories, and (wrote Anthony Buckeridge in *The Author* in 1958) 'the result is the creation of an unrealistic type of school which the reader rejects because it is outside his experience'. It is more remarkable that *The Naughtiest Girl in the School* – which gives a convincing picture of a 'progressive' institution reminiscent in some respects of Curry's Dartington – is the work of a writer generally thought of as prolific rather than original.

It is difficult to estimate Enid Blyton's influence; her two hundred-odd books, of course, cover not only school stories but adventures, religion and Nature Study. Her sales and popularity with younger children are immense. If that is the only criterion (as Captain Johns has maintained) I suppose her books are the best children's books in Britain, if not the world. Few people over ten would seriously suggest that they were. There, is on the contrary, a widespread tendency to dismiss

* But not unknown even in periodicals, e.g. 'Timberlake Co-ed School' in *Girl's Fun*.

them in educational and library circles. One children's librarian spoke to me, with feeling, of their 'intense mediocrity', and Dorothy Neal White, in her otherwise excellent survey, ignores their existence. Other children's writers are loth to criticize. If there are any of us so unworldly as to feel no pangs of envy (and who would not like to know that even in the height of the paper shortage one of his sixteen publishers had allotted sufficient for 250,000 copies of a single title?), at least there is none of us who could hope to escape the suspicion of that human weakness.

The Blyton school stories entertain, but except occasionally, as in *The Naughtiest Girl*, they can hardly be said to go far in depicting reality, stimulating the imagination or educating the emotions. Their style, drained of all difficulty until it achieves a kind of aesthetic anaemia, is the outstanding example of that trend towards semi-basic which we noted in the opening chapter. The exclamation-marks, which often splash across the page like raindrops, suggest the kindergarten teacher telling the story 'with expression'. We can almost hear the voice raised or arrested so as to draw the maximum response from the little listeners. Someone said to me the other day, 'these books are ideal for children – before they can read', and a teacher remarked that their simplicity of style, combined with their entertainment value, made them useful in the early stages of reading, because they broke down the child's resistance to print. Froebelized fiction is a sad symptom of our times, when some children 'resist' that literacy which their grandparents regarded as a prize to be struggled for. If children go on reading such stories long after the age at which they should be getting their teeth into something more nutritious, it is pointless to disparage the author who produces them. It would be more profitable if other authors would set to work and write equally popular books with themes and vocabulary more stimulating to the mental growth of the reader; and if those teachers who seem to imagine that Latin can be learnt by drawing pictures of a trireme could get back to the old-fashioned idea that effort is still, even in modern life, occasionally inescapable.

Even *The Naughtiest Girl* goes to boarding-school. The idea of boarding-school – the escape from at least parental authority, and the companionship of the dormitory – fascinates millions of English children who realize that they have not the slightest chance of experiencing the reality and are thankful, with the more rational part of their minds, that they have not. There was an interesting variation of this fantasy in Phyllis I. Norris's *Meet the Kilburys*. Here the children are mainly day pupils, but have such long journeys from remote villages that Mrs Kilbury hits on the idea of taking a large house and running it for them as a private hostel. There is no suggestion that the authorities should run a school bus or, if the distances are really so great, a publicly-controlled hostel. The only alternative envisaged is that secondary schoolchildren should live in separate lodgings, like undergraduates. Mrs Kilbury feels this to be as undesirable as the reader may feel it to be improbable. So she runs her hostel of twenty-five girls, not to mention half a dozen boys whom she discovers camping unofficially, and for long un-noticed, in her garage.

Now these improbabilities will not spoil the story for the average child. Some of the other elements in the book merit more serious criticism. In these days of Road Safety Campaigns is it responsible to depict a girl mounting a motor-cycle for the very first time in her life and riding it nearly to London? Should her best friend, having failed to restrain her, add to her perils by insisting at least on riding as pillion-passenger? And was it prudent in the circumstances to ride so fast that, in overtaking a car moving at a normal speed, the heroine was able to slow down (as the author makes her) instead of accelerating as is normally necessary? And, since the motor-cyclist is racing the car to London in order to make a business offer, would it not have been more intelligent, as well as safer, to telephone instead? Admittedly Mrs Kilbury was contriving to run her hostel without the convenience of a telephone, but there are call-boxes even in the absurdest stories.

Are these carping criticisms? Surely, if a story purports to be realistic, it should stand the test of common sense. But, someone may complain, you must *have* a story. If you let the girl just telephone, you rob the reader of a whole exciting chapter. Not at all. A writer who knows his job should be able to construct a plot which withstands the tapping hammer of the most captious critic. I know to my cost how often, when planning a story, I have had to say to myself: But they wouldn't *need* to do that, in real life they would be sure to do so-and-so . . . Then either I have had to scrap my first cherished idea, or reconstruct the situation so that the tamer solution is no longer available. The notion that absurdity and impossibility automatically increase entertainment value is a convenient cover for bad craftsmanship.

This story is full of loose ends and coincidences. It has the inevitable pair of twins, a point which will be discussed in the next chapter. There is an element of naïve snobbery. When Lady Pollett-Maynard's children arrive, 'their short skirts and jerseys would never have proclaimed them to be children of rank', which appears to surprise the author unduly. The English has often that stilted quality which is so much worse than the semi-basic. What child would cry: 'Skating! Have you heard any rumour that there is such a possibility?' At the end, the Kilburys solve their financial difficulties by the accidental winning of £1,500 in a crossword competition. (Accidental, because the solution is sent in by another girl, unknown to the one who has actually wielded the pencil.) This sort of *deus ex machina* is bad art and bad morality. We have far too many books, not only school stories, which depend for their happy endings not upon any effort of the characters but upon some lucky improbability. Legacies are left with profusion rare, alas, in our own experience. Lost and stolen articles are restored to grateful owners. Services are rendered and richly rewarded. In so far as all such plots encourage day-dreams of easy money they are bad; when they involve crossword prizes, they are worse. Such competitions, together with football pools, are among the least attractive social phenomena of our time. They will continue so long as the average man finds his own life and work devoid of interest; but one of the aims of children's literature should be to awaken interests in the next generation, so that they will find something more inspiring to do with their evenings than sucking a pencil over an entry-form.

Why pick on this unfortunate book, it may be asked. Many children must have enjoyed it – no less a critic than Margery Fisher, in *Intent Upon Reading*, describes it as 'full of good sense and shrewdness' – and after all there are hundreds of other stories just as bad, or worse. Too true. On those two sad admissions the case for the prosecution rests.

'The school story is a legitimate and desirable form,' I wrote in 1948. 'School looms large in every child's life from the age of literacy onwards, and deserves the same treatment as home and holidays. But if the literary form is to develop it must begin to reflect the new conditions. Someone will tell us at once that the child does not want stories laid in the new Secondary Modern or the Tech. It must be the aged elms and the velvet turf, the mortar-board and the masked intruder, or nothing. Well, you can seldom know that a child will accept a new thing until you have tried, but that is no reason for not trying. Kipling did not write *Stalky* at the request of a juvenile deputation. In actual fact children *have* put the question to me, at National Book League lectures, why aren't there some stories about day-schools like ours? But it is not the author's job to wait for a lead. He should be giving it. The creation of a new secondary school has just the same dramatic possibilities as the creation of a new house, or the revival of a moribund boarding-school, both popular themes in the old tradition. There is just as much potential drama, and infinitely more scope for originality, in depicting the life of any day-school. In an era like this, when we are trying to transform mere school-attendance into that far richer thing, school-life, a handful of good stories might help.'

Since that was written there has been a considerable development. The secondary modern school is the setting for a number of books – C. Day Lewis's brilliant *Otterbury Incident*, E. W. Hildick's *Jim Starling* series, Alice Lunt's *Jeanette's First Term*, and my own *Maythorn* stories. High schools and grammar schools figure in Stephen Tring's *Penny Dreadful* and its sequels,

Anthony Buckeridge's *Rex Milligan* stories (unfortunately a little over-shadowed by his prep-school *Jennings* series, though no wonder, because Jennings is so good), William Mayne's *The Member for the Marsh* (in which he turns from the choristers of *A Swarm in May* to grammar school boys at their week-end avocations), the *Bannermere* books, and (though it is by no means primarily a school story) Anne Bradley's *The Widening Path*. This book, published by the Girl Guides Association in 1952, never attracted the notice it deserved. Its theme was the conflict set up in a girl's mind when a family move, necessitated by her father's work, causes a change of school and Guide Company. It was an interesting book to be published by the Girl Guides Association, because it embodies, along with a lot of other sound ideas, the clear warning that the too-keen Guide runs the danger of becoming a narrow person. 'The widening path' is the heroine's advance towards womanhood. She has to learn, painfully, to adjust herself to a new environment, new interests, new demands, and not least to a new, maturer, relationship with her own parents. It will be a pity if this wise book slips into oblivion.

The same sort of warm humanity pervades Elfrida Vipont's *Lark in the Morn* – a boarding-school story but with a refreshing difference, for it is a Quaker establishment. Antonia Forest, too, though her *Autumn Term* and *End of Term* are set in an 'exclusive' girls' boarding-school, handles this traditional setting with a noteworthy freshness. Mabel Esther Allan gets away from the old conventions in *A School in Danger* and its sequels, laid in Skye. She has also essayed another kind of 'school story', giving children a glimpse of school-life as seen from the blackboard end of the classroom. Her *Judith Teaches* is one of the career books to be considered later, but it may be mentioned here, along with Aubrey de Selincourt's *The Young Schoolmaster*. This book is almost too adult in manner to succeed as a boy's story – I feel that boys old enough to read it are more likely to turn to a full-length novel or, if their interest is practical, to a Ministry of Education hand-out. At the other end of the scale Jacynth Hope-Simpson, in *Danger on the Line*, has drawn a picture of one side of preparatory school life which could be enjoyed by many children under eight, whether or not a boarding-school lies in store for them. This simple little story concerns the narrow-gauge railway which is actually run by the boys of a well-known Herefordshire school. The same school is the setting of her story for older children, *The Man Who Came Back*, but here first-hand observation is subordinated to mystery and almost melodrama, though the unconventional viewpoint – through the eyes of the headmaster's daughter – provides a certain novelty.

CHAPTER TEN

The Family in Fiction

THE normal incidence of twins in Britain is, I have been assured, something like one case in eighty live births. The incidence in fictional families is closer to one in two. There are the Vicarage twins in the *John and Mary* books; more twins in Violet Needham's *The Horn of Merlyns*, Mary Treadgold's *No Ponies*, Erich Kästner's *Lottie and Lisa*, Eleanor Graham's *The Children Who Lived in a Barn*, Malcolm Saville's *Mystery at Witchend*, Eve Garnett's *The Family from One-End Street*, and Heaven knows how many other more recent best-sellers. Everyone knows the 'twins' series by Lucy Fitch Perkins, though few are aware that her original inspiration sprang from the cosmopolitan mixture of children in the Chicago schools, and her desire to promote international understanding. This is just another author I remember if I am told that, when purpose enters a children's story, pleasure flies out. Mrs Perkins had indeed two purposes, not merely to portray the life of another nation, but to add such comment as one would expect from a progressive democrat. Neither of these ulterior motives has prevented her books winning immense popularity, and she has extended her field with titles like *The Spartan Twins* into history. The idea of a 'twin' series on entirely different lines has now been applied to animals by Inez Hogan, whose *Twin Colts*, *Twin Deer* and so forth, besides being really picture-books for the younger child, are not strictly relevant to the present discussion.

My suggestion that the incidence is sometimes as much as one in two is not merely a vague, impatient impression based on a few well-known books. One Christmas I had fourteen girls' stories on my desk simultaneously for review. A swift run-through showed that twins occurred in seven of them. It seemed a shade excessive.

Presumably children like twins. Psychologists tell us that the 'twin fantasy' is very widespread, that children wish they had had a twin and invent one, just as they invent other imaginary playmates. They also show great interest – it has been put to me as strongly as 'fascination' – in such real twins as they happen to know. Here I am at a disadvantage, because I have no recollection of inventing any imaginary playmates, twins or otherwise, in my own childhood; nor, curiously enough, was I personally acquainted with any twins until I once had to teach a brace of Irish boys so nearly alike that it was not until half-term that I observed the mole on one cheek which made identification possible from at least one side of the class-room. It may be felt that this experience embittered me on the subject of twins, but really they were very nice boys and would never exploit their advantage. That exasperation one feels from continually failing to 'spot the lady' was always disarmed by an Irish smile and a helpful: 'Please, sir, *I'm* Maurice.' Unless, of course, it was Desmond.

Authors who use twins are not necessarily aware of this fantasy. Eleanor Graham told me she had never thought very much about it. She had included twins among *The Children Who Lived in a Barn* because it seemed to her a convenient device for introducing two children of the same age. She imagined that most other authors used them for the same reason. That, I suppose, is the great advantage of the twin as an imaginary playmate – other brothers and sisters are necessarily either older or younger, and 'the girl next-door', though one's exact counterpart, cannot be visualized as sharing the same bedroom, an important part of the fantasy. Mrs Perkins probably used twins for her series merely for the same reason as many of us put unrelated boys and girls into our stories, to attract readers of both sexes. Malcolm Saville told me that the twins in his Lone Pine Club were invented purely for entertainment and the closeness of their sympathy exaggerated for this reason. He was not deliberately indulging a particular fantasy.

Twins are seldom introduced for the obvious comic and dramatic possibilities inherent in their resemblance – the reason which attracted Shakespeare in *Twelfth Night* and *The Comedy of Errors*. Their popularity is mainly a modern phenomenon, although Elizabeth Sandham wrote *The Twin Sisters, or the Advantages of Religion* over a hundred and fifty years ago. Boy-twins are not conspicuously less popular than girls, but it is interesting to note that twins occur either in exclusive girls' stories or in those 'family' stories which, while ostensibly catering for both sexes, are generally written by women and read more by girls than by boys. I cannot remember any exclusively boys' book in which twins play an important part. It is not that no lonely boy ever invents a twin for himself, though this perhaps is less common than with girls, because even in these days of feminine emancipation the average boy has still more freedom to rove the district and find flesh-and-blood companions. It is rather that the boy is more interested in action and the girl in personal relationships. It is along these lines that the reading tastes of the two sexes diverge, when they do diverge, and it is obvious in which direction we should look for the twins.

This question is very closely linked with the recent popularity of the 'family' novel in which writers like Kitty Barne and Noel Streatfeild, Eve Garnett and Monica Redlich, have done such good work, or in the 'group' novel involving children of two or three different families, of which Arthur Ransome is the most eminent exponent. The fictional family is an old institution. Charlotte Yonge, who seems for most, if not all, of her seventy-seven years to have been uncertain where babies came from, scatters them prodigally in her stories. Families of eleven and thirteen are typical. She herself was for a long time an only child – her brother came seven years later. 'Every story that she wrote,' said E. M. Delafield, 'was the kind of story that every imaginative child tells itself in one form or another throughout the adolescent years. All such stories represent wish-fulfilment, whether conscious or unconscious. In Charlotte's case, it is quite impossible to miss the implication that her heart's desire was for companionship of her own age, fun, freedom, and such open expression of mutual affection as are natural to early youth.' This is a salutary reminder that the lonely child is not solely a contemporary problem – who could have been lonelier than Mary in Frances Hodgson Burnett's *The Secret Garden*, published in 1911? But it has loomed larger of late, not merely because of the only child but also because of the spaced family. A gap of years (it need not be so many as the seven between the Yonges – I found four sufficient myself) can make a child feel 'only' in many respects.

Now, admitting that these families, groups and twins feed a fantasy which is common among modern children, may we stop a moment and ask one or two questions? First, how far should the author in writing, and the adult customer in buying a children's book, make the satisfaction of this need their aim? We begin to see now why fiction cannot be simply divided into the fantastic (*Aladdin* and *Alice*) and the realistic (*Ballet Shoes* and *Biggles*). Fantasy, in the technical sense, will enter into any kind of story, and into none more than the tale of a family, though the events may be of the homeliest. What we have to decide, in a given plot, is whether the fantasy is a healthy and natural one, and whether it has not been provided for already by innumerable books – whether, in fact, the young reader's imagination could not do with a lead in a new direction, nearer to reality. 'Much material for children,' said a well-known educationist to me recently, 'depends too much on fantasy life whereas it could, and should, make ordinary life exciting and meaningful.'

Secondly, is this special problem of the solitary child best catered for by encouraging this continual self-identification with one of these jolly fictional families who have such wonderful times with tents and caravans, boats and horses? The best books of this *genre* will last as a valuable contribution to children's literature, but one begins to tire of the countless second-rate imitators who have acquired the Ransome formula without the flair. It is sad but certain that the average child reader will never escape from his loneliness by finding such a crew to join in real life – and he must not live all his waking hours in books.

A real problem must have real solutions offered, not only consoling fantasies. We do not want the improbable, accidental solution (thought it occasionally does happen in life), as when the empty house next door is taken by the jolly-looking family who, after some preliminary skirmishes to enhance the drama, take the lonely child into their midst and transform her existence. Nor should we encourage the lonely one to moon about on the off-chance of someone drowning or requiring to be saved from some other predicament, the sequel to which is the dawn of a beautiful friendship. Two things we should do: one is to produce stories pointing the ways which young people can deliberately follow in search of friendship – the joining of Scouts, Guides, Youth Clubs or whatever is appropriate to their age; the second is to remember that we must all expect to be lonely from time to time throughout our lives, and that the capacity first to bear, and then enjoy, a reasonable measure of solitude is one of the most valuable assets a developing personality can acquire. It is for authors to work out how this second idea can be translated into fiction. One way might be for the lonely hero or heroine to develop some special interest which would begin by compensating for the lack of companionship and end by creating it in a natural and probable way – if a boy or girl has an enthusiasm, be it bird-watching or ballet, it is likely sooner or later to bring them into contact with fellow enthusiasts.

The brothers and sisters of juvenile fiction are usually credible. Seldom the parents. It is almost surprising if they are even visible. Parenthood is practically a capital offence. Grandparents are common, but fathers and mothers die young. Who are to be the grandparents in the next fictional generation is a problem which has not yet been faced.

'The basic relationship which children know,' says Mrs White, 'is the parent-child relationship, yet in the majority of tales authors do not even try to handle this theme; they exile father to Poona or despatch him on an expedition, they massacre mothers at child-birth or invalid them for life. Shadowy puppets at best, parents remain in the background, grateful for a brief and tardy appearance in the final chapter, when bearing gifts they return from foreign ports.' If the truth of this estimate does not immediately strike you, it can be tested without reading a single book right through – just take a handful and look at the opening pages. We usually eliminate the parents as a first step. 'Goody,' say the children, 'now you've cleared the ground, we can get on with the adventures.'

As a parent myself I deprecate this practice, but as an author I appreciate its convenience. Apart from technical considerations of story-telling, we are face to face again with one of the basic fantasies. Dr Kate Friedlander speaks of similar fantasies. which show 'the definite strivings of children to become independent of their parents.' (It is comforting to realize that there must be other people's offspring besides mine who burst glowing into the room and announce: 'Patsy and I have had such a lovely game! You and Mummy were dead, and I—') Dr Friedlander goes on: 'This fantasy might give one the idea that the child enjoys being away from home; but experiences during evacuation have shown very clearly that this is by no means so and that when the fantasy "comes true"' (separation, that is, not orphanhood) 'this often leads to severe breakdown in the child. If one is aware of the nature of the fantasy one can easily understand the wide gap between the pleasure of fantasy and its realization.'

Another fantasy-solution is running away from home. 'The amount of running away in children's literature,' says Mrs White, 'is colossal and presents a pretty problem for the child psychologist who can explain these things.' Having no such qualifications, I can offer Mrs White only the most diffident suggestion, that this is another way of escaping in imagination from that parental control against which it is natural, at a certain age, to rebel. Even in the happiest families there can be few children who have never, in a moment of frustration, announced their intention of running away. (Not many parents, however, are confounded by the triumphant question: 'Why shouldn't I? They do in Daddy's books!')

Looking back with some slight embarrassment over the twelve early books written in blissful ignorance that I was the blind agent of a popular fantasy, I find that only in one does the boy-hero grow up without interruption in the normal home environment – and as 'normal' in his case was a Redskin tribe before the coming of the white man readers may not feel that this exception is anything to boast about. In another the children depart, with parental permission, on an improbable but instructive tour of Russia. In the other ten stories there is either permanent or long-term separation from the parents for a variety of reasons. One youth is conscripted at a tender age for a South American war; three are more or less reluctantly driven by the economic conditions of their times; one, I am glad to say, travels for motives of higher education – he is a seventeenth-century New Englander who comes to Oxford and finds himself caught up in the Civil War. Only five can be said to 'run' away in any sense, and of these three, whose hasty impulses have involved them in slaying the King's deer, throwing stones at an enclosing landlord and wounding a Cambridge scholar respectively, flee with the full sympathy of their families and friends as well as of the young reader. A fourth defies a tyrannical father and openly goes off to serve the East India Company. Finally, in one where the parents are dead and the guardians unsympathetic, I attempted (without complete success apparently) to strip the whole project of its glamour, by showing what a modern boy and girl would find themselves up against if they deserted a middle-class home and tried to earn their living in the England of 1935, and by stressing the inevitability of their capture and return.

In real life, for the most part, our children have to live with us and make the best of it, tolerating all those conflicts of personality which the fiction-writer for children hardly dares to mention. *His* parents are perfect, distant or dead. In this respect at least he runs true to the Victorian tradition that a story, whatever else it does, shall not dim the parental halo. This attitude is all very well for the younger child's reading – it would be undesirable to shake his sense of security and faith in adult wisdom – but his own observation and experience will have done this by the time he can read the 'junior novel' type of story. He will need no fiction by then to tell him that parents can be hasty, unjust, selfish and absurd, or that they can disagree, lose their temper and sulk. What he *does* need is fiction which sympathetically handles such characters, and the resultant conflicts between parent and child, parent and parent, so that his understanding is increased and his own problems fall into perspective.

These words, written in 1948, have met with an encouraging amount of support since then. Several authors have in recent years produced stories which grapple with these problems. But it was still possible, early in 1963, for Mr L. Leng, of the University College of North Wales, to tell the Library Association Conference: 'There are too many children's books which carefully skirt around all the facts of life, birth, work, love, marriage, age and death, anything that might arouse strong feelings other than physical courage and physical fear.' It was a librarian's job, he went on, 'to encourage children to read books that would enable them to grow.' He called on them to exclude all books which offered children a false image of human life and false ideas of the rules and values that applied in it. He was, we may presume, attacking not all fantasy but the misleading fantasy which masquerades as reality. 'Children,' he said, 'should not have to unlearn what they have previously been taught.'

Two books for small children are worth mentioning here. Marjorie Flack's *The New Pet* concerns the arrival of a new baby boy and the reactions of his elder brother and sister. The second half of the story, showing how the children adjust themselves to the new situation and how Timmy gradually ceases to be 'it', seems to be admirable, but not all modern parents will agree with the first half. The boy wants a puppy, the girl wants a kitten, but their mother merely smiles and answers: 'Some day soon, I will have the nicest kind of a pet as a surprise for you!' Are children nowadays so often unconscious of their mother's pregnancy – and is it wise to risk their disappointment by making such coy and cryptic promises? By contrast, Margaret

Kornitzer's beautifully illustrated *Mr Fairweather and His Family* handles the difficult theme of the adopted baby with complete success.

Can fiction really help a child in personal difficulties? 'I remember,' wrote Mrs White, 'the tremendous difficulty we had in Dunedin to find a story which would handle the relationship between a stepmother and a stepdaughter in a sympathetic way. The woman who made the request, which was ultimately satisfied by Eliza Orne White's *Farm Beyond the Town*, had found that so many books her stepdaughter read were actually spoiling the relationship between the two of them.' This New England story does not seem to be known in Britain, where perhaps Gwendoline Courtney's *Stepmother* or Alice Lunt's *Secret Stepmother* would meet the need. The relationship is also dealt with in William Mayne's *Underground Alley* and Ruth Adam's awkwardly titled *A Stepmother for Susan of St. Bride's*. From her great experience as a librarian Mrs White suggested only two books which satisfactorily handled the parent-child conflict, Margaret Raymond's *Bend in the Road* and M. I. Ross's *Back of Time*. A subsequently published story is Kitty Barne's *Musical Honours*, in which a family of children (whose mother is dead) face the problem of readjustment with a father who is a returned prisoner of war from the Far East. There is no lack of affection on either side, but the father is necessarily something of a stranger, no less to the elder children who remember him than to the younger who do not. Suffering has hardened him, he has temporarily lost faith in himself as a musician and is trying to adjust himself to a safe commercial career, and, failing to realize how far the children have grown up and developed their own ideas during his long absence, he tries from the worthiest of motives to impose on them his own new-found 'realistic' attitude to music. The plot turns on the various efforts of the children to convince him that they must become musicians and nothing else, and that he too must give up trying to become a business man and go back to the work he loves. There is no need to 'get rid of the parents' when, as in this book, they are such real, recognizable human beings.

What about conflicts between parents? The modern child is all too often aware of them. Wrecked marriages – which eliminate parents in real life much more often than do expeditions to the Brazilian jungle – are taboo in juvenile fiction. Do we hear a chorus of shocked critics? 'Mr Trease would have us drag children's stories down to the sordid level of the Sunday press . . . The seamy side of life will face our young people all too soon – but he would thrust it under their noses in the nursery Well, very few children have nurseries nowadays – and all too many have access to the cheaper Sunday newspapers, anyhow. Most of them know someone at school whose Daddy (or Mummy) doesn't live at home, but is visited with clockwork regularity so many times a year. And even in the happiest and most stable of families a child must be aware of minor frictions. It seems to me about time that this was admitted into stories. Even that pioneer of long ago, Mrs Ewing, as the American librarian, Anne Carroll Moore, has remarked, 'never hesitated to reveal the faults and foibles as well as the virtues of older people in their relations with children.' May we not advance from this point by adding, for the writers of today, the words 'and with each other'?

There seems to be only one serious objection to altering plots and situations away from the over-done fantasies in the direction of reality. Would stories of broken-up marriage, helpful as they might be for that minority of child-readers with painful experience, have a bad effect on the happier majority? Would their sense of security be undermined? Would they start magnifying that parental tiff over the too-hard-boiled egg at breakfast into the beginnings of domestic disaster? It seems unlikely. Provided the situation is handled lightly, without working up a great deal of vicarious emotion, why should a fictional divorce be any more unsettling than a fictional death? Parents have been dying like flies since stories began, but our children still rush off to school in the morning with an undisturbed conviction that we shall survive to grace the supper-table. The cinema presents them with frequent, highly sensational pictures of matrimonial shipwreck, designed for what film-renters conceive to be the adult understanding. Well-written stories for children, with the intention of showing that fathers and mothers do not always get on together, and in extreme cases may feel compelled to separate, will not increase the damage. The important thing is not to overdo the emotional presentation of the theme. The main parental conflict, like the deaths in our present stories, should take place off-stage.

Not that emotion is a bad thing in children's fiction – it is only that it might prove dynamite in the experimental extension of 'family' themes. In general, as Mr Leng implied, poverty of emotion is the saddest flaw in contemporary juvenile books. Restraint and understatement have been carried too far, in understandable reaction from the harrowing death-bed scenes of old-fashioned tales like *St. Winifred's*. But how pleasurably we wallowed in them at the time! Children love pathos, they do not want to be hearty and humorous the whole time, but where are the modern stories which offer the catharsis of a good cry?

Lorna Lewis's *Feud in the Factory* is noteworthy for several reasons. For one thing it gives a vivid picture of industrial life, which is unusual – though Richard Armstrong also does it well in *Sabotage at the Forge* and *The Whinstone Drift*. It starts off by eliminating the parents in traditional style, though the method (an air-raid) was realistic and topical when the story was published. Lorna Lewis has an impish trick of letting you think for a few pages that her story is going off along hackneyed lines of improbability – then she delicately shows you that it isn't. At one point I remember groaning; it looked as though a delightfully realistic novel was to be spoilt by the introduction of mysterious foreign agents and a Fifth Columnist foreman. To my relief, it turned out that the girls (like myself) had jumped to a hasty false conclusion about a perfectly normal incident. No doubt (like myself) they had read too many sensational stories. This is a book of twentieth-century life, about adolescent girls who smoke rather sooner than their elders approve, put on plenty of make-up and knock back a glass of cider or two at the Works dance. But its relevance here lies in its handling of the parents' death theme. The two sisters have just been reminded of their dog which also perished in the air-raid, and one says:

'Why is it we cry so much over poor little Andrew and hardly ever over Mother and Father?'

Rosie thought. 'It's odd. I don't really know. P'r'aps it's because Andrew was part of our games and always went everywhere with us, and now he doesn't, while Mother and Father we just think of as being away for a holiday and miss in that way. I mean in a way we've hardly taken in yet that, that—'

She stopped, and Joan said quickly: 'That's it. Let's stop talking about it. Come on, we'll make jam sandwiches . . .'

Contrast that typical modern restraint with Louisa Alcott's treatment of the father's illness in *Little Women*. A similar theme – family-life disrupted by father's illness – has been particularly

well handled by Monica Redlich. Her *Five Farthings* tells how
Mr Farthing had to go into a London hospital for lengthy
treatment and the family had to adjust themselves to a complete
change of home, schools and general existence. Mother, for a
start, goes back to her old job at Swan and Edgar's. This is a
good story of Mother and the children grappling with a sudden
rush of new problems, and it would have been no worse if the
same situation had arisen from a different cause not uncommon
in everyday existence.

The useful uncle and the accommodating aunt loom larger
in the story-book family than in real life. They have almost
entirely superseded the wicked uncle exemplified in *Richard III*
and *The Babes in the Wood*. They are childless but child-loving.
They embody all the grown-up advantages – they are knowledgeable about navigation and handy with horse-drawn
caravans – but they have none of that tiresome fussiness which
goes with parents. The useful uncle is never married to the
accommodating aunt, for that would distract him from his
essential function of helping the young people whenever their
problems call for adult assistance. The aunt, indeed, is usually
segregated in a book by herself. It is her function to live in
remote and interesting places, as in *The House on the Cliffs* by
Rita Coatts, where her nephews and nieces can stay with her
and chase smugglers or solve mysteries during the hols. These
aunts are as unbelievably hospitable as the uncles are skilful –
they frequently invite, for long periods, children whom they
have never seen. 'An unknown and elderly aunt had invited
her to stay with her for two or three months,' declares a typical
story-teller on the first page of the book. Auntie is more often
younger, but her character is almost invariably a pleasant
surprise. She knows just what children like to eat and do, she is
never fussy or conventional, she is in short 'not a bit like a
grown-up'. No higher compliment could be paid.

Uncles and aunts divide the honours fairly evenly in the tale
of everyday life in England. In the adventure story the uncles
have it. They provide the expeditions in search of Inca treasure

or uranium deposits. They are the professors, occupying vague chairs in unspecified universities, who are able to leave their academic duties to fly space-ships to the moon. Even in death they are good for one more adventure. Never having married they have money to leave, and to whom should they leave it but the boy-hero and his crooked cousin? 'By the terms of their wealthy uncle's will . . .' begins the blurb of a typical story, and sure enough the characters are in the African bush before they can say 'probate'.

The avuncular fantasy (if such is known to the science of psychology) scarcely requires very searching examination. The child is struggling for independence. Reason tells him that the story would be too glaringly impossible for acceptance if no adult took part, and instinct chimes in that it is very handy to have the adult there to take over when the situation gets really out of hand. He wants to have his cake and eat it. Independence plus help, advice and reassurance when wanted, but not before. No parent need apply.

It is all very natural and harmless, though not very realistic. The constant repetition of the device probably does not bore the child so much as it does the adult critic. Authors who have used it in more than ten books might like to exercise their ingenuity and invent some noticeable variation.

CHAPTER ELEVEN

Home and Holiday

'ENGLAND,' we have already quoted Paul Hazard as saying, 'could be reconstructed entirely from its children's books.' He did not of course mean that the real life of the country was to any extent depicted there. Any social historian, writing a thousand years hence with no data but a few tons of pre-1950 'juveniles' unearthed from the British Museum vaults, would reconstruct a very peculiar island indeed. Nearly all children, he would deduce, attended boarding-schools. Such parents as survived their birth (and fatherhood was just as dangerous as maternity) were vaguely professional. People usually lived in Hampshire, so that ponies could be kept, or, if they were Londoners, they went to Exmoor for the holidays. The classless society had, in a sense, been already achieved: all the main characters were comfortably middle-class (some parents had a careless habit of 'losing all their money' in some unspecified manner, but this did not affect their status because they always recovered it in the last chapter); there might be an occasional Lord, just as there would be friendly and informative grooms and fishermen, but these minor characters hardly disturbed the impression that all real people were neither vulgarly rich nor tiresomely poor. One book, Eve Garnett's *Family from One End Street*, the historian would probably discount as a puzzling forgery, or an allegory whose point escaped him. In the face of all the other evidence how could this story of a dustman's family bear any relation to reality – where the mother washed clothes for other people, and the children sat for free places at day schools, played on the waste ground by the canal, and went to the seaside by train?

Paul Hazard was far too shrewd to imply any such thing. He meant that we could reconstruct not the external life of

England, but the subcutaneous pattern of its ideals and aspirations, its written traditions and its unspoken taboos.

The outstanding literary landmark of this period is Arthur Ransome. His name will go into the short list of writers like Talbot Baines Reed, who have deflected the stream of fiction into new channels. What Reed did for the school term Dr Ransome did for the holidays. As the holidays scarcely existed for Reed, so school plays no part in the Ransome world. We have already seen that the school story, especially for boys, had received no great new impetus for several decades; it was already flagging when this new voice cried: 'What about the holidays?' and flung open the door upon a fresh view.

It is a fantasy world, disguised under a wealth of realistic practical detail. These children who run through the whole series, *Swallows and Amazons*, *The Coot Club* and the rest of them, whether the scene is the Norfolk Broads, the Lake District or the Hebrides, are practical beyond all else. They hammer, paint, cook, navigate, stow hammocks and swab decks. Their favourite reading is maps and charts, and they write mainly in logbooks. The dialogue is in keeping:

> 'Stern warp, John! Haul in and belay!'
> 'Aye, aye, Sir.'
> 'Port warp, Nancy.'

The child who has read and re-read *Great Northern*, not to mention its predecessors, should be just about qualified to sit for his master's ticket. Yet it is a fantasy world in that the child-group is almost independent of adult interference. There is only the benevolent uncle to play his familiar role. In *Swallows and Amazons* a parent authorizes a venture afloat in the telegram which reads: 'Better drowned than duffers.' It is an attitude commoner in fiction than in life.

Arthur Ransome's contribution must not be minimized. Though sometimes in the past uncritically revered, his books are solid and genuine. He writes of the things he cares about, he does not 'cater'. He demonstrates, over and over again, that the interest of the child can be held without introducing improbable sensations. In *Great Northern* the whole drama is built round the nest of a rare bird, and the villain is nothing more sinister than a vulgar and unscrupulous egg-collector. Ransome does not need to 'bring in the police', because he can manage without that element of crime which so many authors (or perhaps, so many publishers) believe to be an essential ingredient of an enjoyable fictional holiday. Handiness, co-operation, decent behaviour and above all self-reliance ('better drowned than duffers') – these are the Ransome virtues, and very well worth preaching they are, especially when the writer never falls for a phrase or syllable into a recognizable preacher's tone.

All these things are excellent. It would be ungracious to expect more of any single writer. Unfortunately some of his admirers – probably to his own vexation more than to anybody else's – used to talk as though the Ransome books represented a kind of final, highest-attainable pinnacle in the range of juvenile fiction. Nothing could be less helpful to arriving at a fair estimate of their worth, and nothing more unjust to writers in other fields. There is a breezy healthiness about his stories which at times is suspiciously suggestive of antiseptic. These children are so busy hauling in and belaying that they seem untroubled by dreams or problems of personal relationship. They take plenty of soundings at sea, but they plumb no emotional depths. Arthur Ransome himself, who once turned aside to collect Russian fairy-tales, knows well enough that the world of his own stories is only one world. He who, as a young newspaper correspondent, witnessed the Bolshevik Revolution, is only too well aware of wider horizons than are scanned by his young voyagers.

What Ransome has done with boats, other very competent writers have done with bicycles, ponies, horse-caravans, houseboats, tents, cottages, and again with sailing-boats. Peter Dawlish, writing with a long experience of the sea, and ably assisted by P. A. Jobson, a marine artist, as illustrator, started a popular series with *'Dauntless' Finds Her Crew*. *Dauntless* is a derelict French fishing-smack, which the boys (with just enough benevolent grown-up guidance) recondition with a zest and efficiency worthy of Ransome characters. *Dauntless* had a prototype in real life, and the illustrations were based on her. Actuality is the hallmark of these writers – Garry Hogg, for instance, took a cabin-cruiser and a party of young people on a long trip round the canals and up the Thames before starting *Explorers Afloat*, and his earlier book, *Explorers Awheel*, was the fruit of many cycle-tours in his own boyhood. One is grateful to this book because it puts in a word for the humble bicycle, which is still, for millions of children, the only means of faring forth in search of adventure. David Severn, M. E. Atkinson, and Malcolm Saville were perhaps the other three outstanding pioneers of the holiday theme, if we except the 'riding school' of writers, who constitute such a phenomenon that they had better be considered separately.

'Of course,' a well-known publisher once said to me 'Ransome merely discovered a new formula. Once the others found it, there was nothing to it. Everyone's using it now.' That, I should say, was much less than the truth. There *have* been many imitators and a number of writers, like those mentioned above, who have been consciously or unconsciously influenced by him. (They may not have read a line of his books, but influences are subtle things, operating at second- and third-hand.) The fact remains that in his own field Arthur Ransome has no equal. He created a new *genre* and perfected it in the fifteen years from 1932 (*Peter Duck*) to 1947 (*Great Northern*). Can anybody else do much more with it? And if the answer is No, we had better ask ourselves the next question: *Where do we go from here?*

Not into the stables, anyhow. It is time that door was locked for a season.

Shortly before the first star of the Ransome constellation glittered above the horizon, another portent appeared, less brilliant in itself but of no less astrological significance. It was *Moorland Mousie*, written under the pseudonym 'Golden Gorse'. It was, in a sense, an animal-book like *Black Beauty*, for it was a

West Country story narrated by a pony. It was the founder
of the new 'riding school' of children's fiction, a form of
literature now so all-pervasive that this chapter might almost
be entitled 'Gymkhana and Jodhpur'.

Let me say quickly, before the riding-crops of indignant
enthusiasts rain upon my shoulders, that I have nothing against
the pony story as such. It is pleasant to see a generation trans-
ferring its enthusiasm from high-powered machines to some of
the most attractive of the domestic animals. I was glad to see
my daughter's delight in riding, and thankful that all problems
of present-giving were solved for several birthdays in succession
by the variety of objects – yellow ties with foxes' heads on them,
crops, gloves, and so forth – without which it appears that a
pony cannot be enjoyably ridden. But if this enthusiasm had
deepened into an obsession, so that she had become blind to
other interests, I should have been very sorry indeed. That
the fantasy of possessing a pony (or two, or three) had become
something like an obsession in many children's minds could in
those days be seen from any book department. Typical titles
were *Wish for a Pony*, *I Wanted A Pony*, *I Had Two Ponies*, *Three
Ponies and Shannan*, *A Pony for Jean*, *Another Pony for Jean*, *More
Ponies for Jean*, and (highest bid so far) *Six Ponies*. The main
thing was to get the word into your title – even if, like the
ingenious Mary Treadgold, you called your book *No Ponies*.
(The young hippomaniacs knew perfectly well that the ponies
would turn up somewhere in the book.) Almost any book,
irrespective of quality, was sure of a considerable sale if the
title included that magic word. Some children would have
demanded Shakespeare's *Richard III* if it had been put in the
right dust-jacket and renamed *A Pony for Richard*.

Some of these books went a long way in the encouragement
of wealth fantasy. Diana Pullein-Thompson's *Three Ponies and
Shannan* is concerned with the poor little rich girl who has three
expensive ponies and every facility for keeping them (or rather
having them kept) in perfect condition. She just cannot help
winning all the pots at the gymkhana, and wonders why the
other children, the poor creatures with only one pony apiece,

are not very friendly towards her. But the best example was perhaps *I Had Two Ponies*, by Josephine Pullein-Thompson. The social milieu is indicated in the second paragraph:

> Daddy's business in India wasn't being run properly and, as he is the sort of person who believes that if you want a thing done properly you must do it yourself, he had decided to go out and put the matter right. Mummy, who was bored and thought a change of scene would be nice, was going with him . . . Nanny was the only person who sympathized with me; she said that now Daddy was a Lord he oughtn't to demean himself by bothering about business and that if she was in his place *she* would wash her hands of it. But then she could hardly be expected to approve, because Mummy had decided that this was an opportune moment to give her notice.

Nanny is not the only victim of the purge. Daddy 'sacked Charles, the footman, who always became nervous at dinner-parties and dropped or clattered the crockery, and the head gardener, because he had never been able to grow carnations.' The ponies are sold – Christabel doesn't care much, because, she tells us, 'I must confess, and, in my imagination I hear your gasps of horror, that I never really liked riding. Perhaps rides accompanied by Small, our groom, on Daydream, or on Daddy's hunter, King Cole, were not very amusing, but I think really that I was just rotten to the core.' The theme of the story is, of course, her moral regeneration.

Meanwhile the ponies are sold, and Small goes the way of the hapless footman and head gardener. We cannot, from the text, compile a complete census of the staff at Bramblewick Hall, but we hear of Monk, Mummy's lady's maid, and Dale, Daddy's valet, both bound for India with their employers, and there is some discussion as to whether Cook should also be placed on the overseas draft. 'Daddy said that an Indian cook would be quite adequate, but Mummy said that she was going to give dozens of dinner-parties and that she was sure that the Indian wouldn't know enough dishes.' Money is no object at Bramble-wick Hall. The schoolgirl heroine mentions her own expensive radiogram 'which, among other things, my parents had given me for Christmas'.

This book is quite amusingly written. Miss Pullein-Thompson's equestrian knowledge is presumably impeccable – it is in most pony-books and has to be. A certain amount of technical information, with sound views on the treatment of horses and courtesies expected of the well-bred rider, is admirably instilled into the reader. There are the inevitable twins, but the author compensates for this by one more original feature: some of her child characters not only read books, they even write. It is a curious thing how many other authors, who depend for their public on book-loving children, depict characters who are never seen with a book in their hands and might be taken for hearty illiterates, were it not for their skill in deciphering codes.

No Mistaking Corker, by Monica Edwards, is pure escapism, but on a lower income-level. Mother goes no farther than 'Aunt Bea at Cannes'. After all, she has had her appendix out. The children go on a riding-tour from their country house in Hampshire to Granny's in Dorset. Father is actually allowed to go with them – someone has to drive the horse-caravan with all the gear, and no uncle seems available. Miss Edwards has now about twenty such books to her credit. They are pleasantly evocative of the countryside, especially Romney Marsh, and in the view of at least one County Library (Hertfordshire) 'should help the pony-mad child to take a broader view of life'.

The pony-stories of the well-known novelist Joanna Cannan (mother of the three Miss Pullein-Thompsons – for there are books by Christine Pullein-Thompson also in the same *genre*) contain much humour and acute observation and seem free from the implicit snobbery and excessive fantasy which mar so many of such tales. Mary Treadgold's too, with their glimpses of the Channel Islands or the South of France, have something more in them than mere hippomania. A pleasant little book which deserves to be more widely known is Priscilla Warner's *Biddy Christmas*, in which (for a change) the heroine has to overcome her fear and dislike of ponies. In this story, again, the interest is by no means confined to the quadrupeds – young readers can learn something about themselves and human relations at the same time. The group of books which Katharine Hull and Pamela Whitlock began to write as school-girls – *The Far Distant Oxus* and the rest – have a fleck of that same youthful fire and imagination that we find in *Bevis*. The list of pony-books could be lengthened almost indefinitely with the works of Primrose Cumming, Gillian Baxter, M. E. Atkinson, and many more. Well might the bookseller cry with Macbeth: 'What! Will the line stretch out to the crack of doom?' It is worth noting that Miss Diana Pullein-Thompson has in the past few years turned to fresh fields with considerable success. The old love of animals provides the theme for both *The Boy and the Donkey* and *The Secret Dog*, but the characters are working-class (one boy, in the second story, is a West Indian), the milieu is shabby back-street London, and there is a warm, down-to-earth quality running through from first page to last.

It will be noted that almost all pony books are written by women and appeal primarily to girls, a rare exception being David Severn's *Ponies and Poachers*. R. S. Summerhays, a riding expert, has pointed out in an article in the girls' annual, *Discovery and Romance*, 1946, that 'this closely knit tie' between horse and rider 'seems to be most conspicuous with the young women of today. It is so evident that it amounts to a minor phenomenon.' It is '. . . always daughters, for sons don't seem to get bitten by this horse-fly. The girls outnumber the boys to such an extent that the latter are negligible.' As with riding, so with the stories about it.

The most curious thing of all is that the pony book is immensely popular with many children who do not ride. Librarians in grimy London boroughs have told me of the demand from girls who never even see a horse, except between the shafts of a dray. I am assured that there is a Freudian explanation. But then there always is.

Boys of course appear in the pony book. There is little segregation of the sexes in this or in any other type of holiday story. We have moved a long way since 1935 when a *B.O.P.*

editor, commissioning an article on a Young Pioneer camp in the Crimea, asked me if it would be possible to write it without mentioning that half the Pioneers were female. Even now, in other branches of fiction, there is some resistance to the girl character. 'The modern boy,' Captain Johns once told me, 'knows what he wants and he will strive to get it. Of course, this has nothing to do with sex. Boys hate the introduction of a girl into their stories. On the other hand, girls always have an eye on the matrimonial possibilities.' I am not sure that the modern boy *does* hate the introduction of girls, even into the adventure story. One naturally hesitates to challenge the judgement of a best-selling author like the creator of Biggles, but I have put the question to many schoolboy audiences, and in most cases (not all) the show of hands has revealed a large majority of favour of admitting heroines as well as heroes.

How should the boy and girl relationship be handled, either in the holiday story or in any other? There was always a rigid taboo against heterosexual emotion in our juvenile fiction, though there were some powerful homosexual undercurrents in the early school stories, of which writers and readers seemed about equally unconscious until the Wilde case opened their eyes. The relationship between boys and girls is still often represented by the modern writer as a natural, 'healthy' association in which sex plays no part and sexual differences are ignored. To make the girl characters acceptable to the boy readers, authors long ago created a type of girl (developed out of the old-fashioned tomboy) who can ride, swim and climb as well as her brothers, and so commands the respect of his friends. The distinctively feminine interests and attributes are played down.

It seems questionable whether this is the ideal method. We all know now that a child's sexual interests begin many years earlier than it was once customary to admit, and to this psychological discovery has been added, since the war, remarkable if not unanimous evidence of the earlier physical maturation of both boys and girls. Yet some children's authors still like to think that eighteen or thereabouts is the age of awakening. They sometimes introduce, as minor characters, elder brothers and sisters who get engaged as part of the sub-plot – and these issues are certainly handled with more sympathy nowadays, and less of the old fashioned, uncomprehending contempt revealed in Richmal Crompton's *William* stories. A present-day boy of William's age (strictly speaking William is ageless, but I suppose we may visualize him as about eleven?) is probably writing love-letters to someone at the Girls' High School, and being answered that she is willing to be friends 'but nothing more'. In real life today William and Ginger would spend more of their time making such dates and less of it in repeating the monotonous pattern of stock farcical situations. All those expeditions, too, which our other authors describe – those

campings and voyagings and caravannings – would be shot through and through with usually innocent and harmless, but just as definitely sexual and emotional, relationships.

Writing of the co-educationsl method in his book, *Education for Sanity*, W. B. Curry drew attention to the harm that can be done by 'the notion that a brother and sister comradeship is the ideal relationship between the sexes'. That is precisely the notion that is plugged steadily in all these stories.

It may seem the function of a kill-joy to remind children that life is not all holidays, but even the most ardent admirer of escapist fiction could hardly stigmatize writers like Noel Streatfeild, Kitty Barne, Eleanor Graham, Monica Redlich and Lorna Lewis, as kill-joys. Each of them puts fun, excitement, sometimes a dash of mystery, into her stories, but each is primarily interested in the reality of everyday life – the struggle to make a living or to keep a home together or both. *Ballet Shoes* is the tale of three child performers whose earnings are badly needed to help with the housekeeping. *Musical Honours* is a story of family readjustments and the choice of careers. *The Children Who Lived in a Barn* is concerned with the eldest sister's battle to keep together her family of presumed orphans against the well-meaning but disruptive forces wishing to separate and adopt them. In *Five Farthings*, as already mentioned, Father is in hospital, Mother is back at work in a West End store, and the children have to adjust themselves to new schools or jobs, and a transformed existence in a flat over a shop on Ludgate Hill. *Feud in the Factory* shows the orphaned sisters trying to make a home for themselves. All these writers present a gay, courageous picture of everyday life under difficulties – it is typified in the title of another Lorna Lewis story dealing with the blitz, *Tea and Hot Bombs* – but the critic will divine in their work an underlying seriousness which will never obtrude itself upon the young reader.

Of this group I approached the late Kitty Barne with my blunt question, why did she write for children? Her reply was brief enough to be quoted almost in full:

I think the writers of children's novels, which is the sort of book I write, can never feel so happily irresponsible as the writer for grown-ups whose minds are presumably formed. Inaccurate facts, badly-observed backgrounds and false emotions are more dangerous for children who swallow them down wholesale in the realistic sort of story and believe them. They still have a respect for the printed page – 'I saw it in a book, so it's true.' It's a serious thing to put a twelve-year-old wrong in either his values or his facts.

I think the reason I began to write novels for children was because I enjoyed them – as I continue to do. There is an exhilaration in writing for boys and girls just as there is in being with them.

As for 'saying anything to the rising generation' my view is that if the book has been enjoyable and if the problems the characters have to face are real, small-scale maybe but not trivial in a child's life, then it probably has said something to the reader ... My own belief is that children don't mind long words or ideas that are a little big for them – they apprehend even if they don't comprehend; and with many writers there is apt to be too much patronising simplicity and far too much 'brightness'.

Nearly all books of this type have one problem in common – that of careers. Whatever else the characters are up against, the adolescent members of the family are looking ahead to the work they want – or will have – to do. And, very rightly, the emphasis is put on the 'want'.

The career-story, whether in biography or in the pure fiction form of a junior novel, can be one of the most valuable additions to our shelves. If there is one pathetic, infuriating spectacle it is that of a boy or girl who (as often as not after the most expensive education that money can buy) still has no definite interest in any particular career. That any adolescent should need to be questioned on the subject and should expect suggestions to be laid down before him for approval (and how familiar such family conferences are!) is an implied indictment of all the educational processes which have gone before. A good deal is done now to prevent this 'don't-know-what-I-want' attitude from developing. There are 'careers masters', there are visits to factories and newspaper-offices and farms, there are psychological tests to detect special aptitudes, there is good advice offered from many quarters . . . And it may well be, for some children, that the way ahead is pointed by some story which has gripped their imagination.

Every library should have as many good career-novels as it can lay hands on. There are not so very many even now. When this section was originally written it was possible to compile a short list of individual stories which contained a strong documentary element, Noel Streatfeild's *Ballet Shoes* being perhaps the classic example. There were other stage books such as Helen Dore Boylston's *Carol* series, Pamela Brown's *The Swish of the Curtain* and its sequels, and Arnold Haskell's *Felicity Dances*. There were the popular *Sue Barton* nursing stories, of which Dorothy Neal White declared: 'If the hospital boards of New Zealand want a new method of overcoming the shortage of nurses, they could easily ensure a stream of recruits for the next ten years by buying hundreds of copies and distributing them to every girls' school in the country. A vocational guidance officer recently pointed out that the chronicles of Sue's career have attracted more girls to nursing than all the milk-and-water accounts of Florence Nightingale which are presumed by the aged to be such efficient propaganda for the profession.'

In general these early career-novels dealt with the superficially glamorous professions, whether or not the treatment helped to strip away some of the glamour. The conception of a comprehensive career-series, to cover a variety of occupations, planned and commissioned with deliberate social intention, had only just emerged in the late nineteen-forties with the publication, by the Oxford University Press, of J. S. Arey's medical story, *Students at Queen's*, and Peter Dawlish's *The First Tripper*, about the Merchant Navy. Since then, other publishers have followed this lead, notably the Bodley Head, with a long all-feminine list (career-fiction seems on the whole less popular with boys, who get their inspiration either direct from life or from more technical literature), and Chatto and Windus who, like Oxford, cater for readers of both sexes. Most of these books are reliable enough as an introduction to the subject in question – no adolescent is likely to plunge into a career without seeking further information from other sources, and the story-teller has played his part if he has aroused interest and stimulated such inquiry. The literary quality of such volumes inevitably varies immensely. Some are by expert story-tellers, who can be relied upon to overcome, in a large degree, the limitations imposed by the documentary form. Lorna Lewis has written *June Grey: Fashion Student*, *Valerie: Fashion Model*, and *Judy Bowman: Therapist*; Monica Edwards, *Joan Goes Farming* and *Rennie Goes Riding*; Laurence Meynell, *Policeman in the Family* and *The Young Architect*; Shirley Darbyshire, *Sarah Joins the W.R.A.F.*; and Mabel Esther Allan not only *Judith Teaches*, already mentioned elsewhere, but a nursery-school story, *Here We Go Round*. Other books have been commissioned on the strength of the writer's inside knowledge rather than of literary skill. Sometimes, because sincerity and enthusiasm have a way of coming through, a readable story has resulted. Sometimes not.

The very word 'career' still carries something of a middle-class flavour, though considerably weakened by the levelling up of educational and social opportunities which has taken place in recent years. Say what we will, a career implies at least a minimum of foresight, ambition, training and responsibility. It will always be for the abler child, and if he succeeds in it he will soon cease to regard himself as 'working-class', whatever his family-origins. With a few exceptions, the career-novels are not going to be of great interest to the innumerable boys and girls who may feel pretty sure that they are never going to have careers, but only jobs.

It has frequently been complained that the interests of such children are ignored by the story-teller, that there are 'no working-class stories for children', and this complaint applies of course to the whole range of fiction. The school story, as we have seen, has only recently discovered the world of the asphalt playground. The holiday adventure has too often been built round what a Manchester teacher told me were scornfully dismissed by his pupils as 'egg-head' activities, such as bird-

L

watching and archaeology. Such generalizations are tricky. Television and other mass media – not to mention the inspired work of devoted individual teachers – have done much to introduce all kinds of children to the 'egg-head activities'. Continental travel is now a familiar experience for the young people of my own Herefordshire village and boys from a near-by secondary modern school carry out canoe-journeys down the Wye which might well inspire an Arthur Ransome to chronicle them. My newspaper tells me of a Welsh child's excitement at finding a Celtic sword turned up by her father's plough – and of Borstal boys enthusiastically helping with an archaeological dig in Lincolnshire. But we all know what the Manchester teacher meant. The world of the mean streets and the canal towpath and the slag heaps, the world of so many children so much of the time, has been too little reflected in juvenile literature.

There were various reasons for this neglect. Few authors wanted – or were able – to write that kind of book. They were themselves solidly middle-class and wrote of the world they knew, the kind of children they had been themselves. When the working-class threw up a writer, he might become a novelist, a playwright or a poet, but seldom if ever, from the time of D. H. Lawrence down to that of Alan Sillitoe, was he impelled to write children's books. Had he done so, he would have met with scant encouragement from publishers. Books, he would have been warned, were something bought by middle- and upper-class parents. They wanted their children to read about nice people of equal or superior social standing. Low-life had no legitimate place in children's literature. It was argued, on the analogy of the cinema, that even the working-class would be likely to prefer escapist fantasies, but as such people never entered bookshops there was little point in considering their tastes anyhow.

Today, the expansion of the public library service and the creation of school and form libraries throughout the educational system have completely transformed the position. As Ian Serraillier wrote in *The Author* in 1958: 'The children's classics seem to have been written for upper middle-class children from bookish and leisured homes. Today readership and reading ability are much more varied. There are four or five times as many secondary modern school children as grammar school ones, and their needs are different.' In the same issue E. W. Hildick wrote: 'Hitherto, the British juvenile novel has been largely a preserve of the middle classes – a literature about, by and for them. Year after year, troops of well-spoken child protagonists have goshed and golleyed their way through holiday adventures in a world where the Broads are O.K. but Blackpool and Butlin's unmentionable.' Edward Blishen ended his own contribution to the discussion: 'Teacher-librarians pray for a revolution in the sphere of children's fiction similar to that which has occurred since the war in the sphere of their non-fiction. Huck, to put it briefly, has become a reader of books. But most of the books are written for Tom Sawyer.'

Whether or not we have yet had a revolution on a scale to satisfy Mr Blishen's teacher-librarians, no one can any longer pretend that there is no working-class fiction for children. We have seen how Mr Hildick and others have put the Council School firmly on the map. Out-of-school activities – especially the life of the back-street gang – are covered in an ever-lengthening list of books. Jo Hatcher's *The Gasworks Alley Gang Goes West* may be far-fetched but it is amusing. *The Racketty Street Gang*, a story of the Australian waterfront by L. H. Evers, will help British children to recognize their opposite numbers in another country. So will Paul Berna's *A Hundred Million Francs*, where the gang's territory lies in the backstreets of Paris, and Harry Kullman's *The Secret Journey*, in which a middle-class boy goes adventuring into those slums which we are so often assured do not exist in Sweden. Frederick Grice's *The Bonny Pit Laddie* is a brilliant re-creation of the bad old days in the Durham coalfield, when strikers could be evicted from company cottages and their furniture dumped in the street – though it practically qualifies also as an historical story I would put this at, or near, the top of any list of working-class children's books. One of the

new towns is the setting for Barbara Willard's *Eight for a Secret*.
Anne Barrett's *Songberd's Grove*, Elizabeth Stucley's *Magnolia
Buildings*, Marjorie A. Sindall's *The Budds of Paragon Row*, and
Ann Thwaite's *The House in Turner Square* are all stories of the
shabbier city streets, like the two stories by Diana Pullein-
Thompson previously mentioned, and Joan Selby-Lowndes'
Family Star is set in a London mews. William Mayne's *Summer
Visitors*, despite its background in the Yorkshire dales, is about
schoolboy campers from a northern industrial area.

With these and a number of other titles which could be added,
the new reader can hardly be said to be neglected. No one is
suggesting, let us hope, that in going out to meet the new reader
the author has got to limit his themes to those which lie within
the child's immediate interest and experience – or that, because
the grammar-school stream children are outnumbered four or
five to one by the less bookish children, the output of stories
should be planned, numerically and in linguistic complexity,
to the same ratio. The less bookish children will never want,
child for child, anything like as many stories to read. They must
have enough, yes. Their special interests must be borne in mind,
and their special difficulties. There must be simpler stories,
there must be stories so simple that they can be enjoyed by the
backward reader. But all this is an educational matter – extremely
important, but distinct from the literary problem which should
always remain the writer's central concern. He is glad to be an
entertainer if he can, delighted to be an educator if the schools
find him useful, but his real function is to be a literary artist,
and if he fails in that he fails completely.

So, with respect, he must continue to write for the bookish
child. Not the grammar-school child or the middle-class child
(enough of whom, heaven knows, are semi-literate Philistines)
but for any child, whatever his school grade or his father's
income-group, who has learnt to surrender to the magic of a
well-told tale. In so writing, he will welcome his new-found
freedom to depict new themes and settings and characters and
modes of speech, but he will not fall into the error of supposing
that the reader from the tenement or the Council house is

interested only in seeing the realities of his own life reflected. An author's function is not solely to hold up mirrors – it is his job also to open windows, windows with long views and in many different directions.

CHAPTER TWELVE

To You – For Action

'NO one will agree with all that has been said,' I wrote fifteen years ago. 'In the foregoing pages it is inevitable that some toes have been trodden on, but that is usually a sure way to start people talking. And discussion – intelligent discussion, based not only on nostalgic memories but on reading of current books and observation of contemporary children – is something that we have never really had on this subject, at least in Britain. If we were only agreed that this topic deserved and demanded such discussion, then this book, however glaring its omissions, unfair its comments and wrongheaded its conclusions, would at least have fulfilled its primary purpose. But an author must optimistically assume that many readers will agree with much that he has said, and it is to these that the final chapter is addressed.'

As it turned out, the volume of agreement came as a pleasant surprise. Letters of enthusiastic support reached me from publishers and parents, teachers, librarians, even fellow-authors to whose work I had been far from complimentary. I could almost see swords leap from their scabbards and bonfires blaze from hill to hill. The truth is, I imagine, that the first publication of the survey coincided happily with an already-stirring interest in the subject which chose that moment for sudden eruption. Certainly it would be impossible to complain today that there has been no intelligent discussion. Children's literature figures regularly in the programmes of parent-teacher associations, training colleges, university education departments, courses for school librarians and teachers in general, and all kinds of other gatherings from literary societies to Women's Institutes. We may hope that the day is not far off when the extent of public interest will be reflected in more generous treatment on radio and television, now that an increasing number of people recognize the problem as important, if not from the literary at least from the social point of view.

Eleanor Graham had already written a challenging article in *Junior Bookshelf* in July, 1944:

> The war has focused attention on public morals, the miserable degeneration in our social and religious outlook, and the rapidly developing atrophy of genuine affection and real home life. Lastly the Education Bill and related literature urge quality in education while putting forth a plea for better books to supply a fuller background of general knowledge, to open doors and to beckon the child out of the rut into which he or she has been born.
>
> How are we standing up to all these new issues? Are we still satisfied with the familiar pre-war formula for a 'good modern story' – to get rid of the parents, divorce the children from home surroundings and influence, and, in an atmosphere of artificial freedom, to project them into a succession of thrilling adventures, very unlikely to occur in real life? The implication has been that home was boring, happy family life improbable, dull, or at best a sentimental idea. Any picture of religion as an integral part of the background of childhood (unless dealt with as a quaint survival) has grown to be regarded as in doubtful taste and likely to prejudice sales. The formula surely has a part to play in the emancipation of children's literature from the falsity of Victorian influence, but surely also only a part in the evolution of a still better phase – one in which truth and integrity are all important, and pictures of real life vital in all the infinite variety of human experience, domestic and scientific, universal as well as local; a phase also in which we shall not lose sight of the importance of fantasy, appreciating the important lessons in philosophy and human understanding which are implicit in all true fairy tales.

What has been and can be done to help on that 'still better phase' to which she looked forward? Discussion is idle unless it points to action, and in this case there is something which every reader of these words can do, be he writer or artist, publisher or editor, librarian or teacher, parent or real-life bachelor uncle. It may be refreshing to some to see that I do not include the

Government. Their help is welcome enough in such matters as educational expenditure on books and the promotion of our literature abroad through the British Council, but in the choice of what is printed let them not meddle.

Government censorship has always attracted some people as a short cut to the solution of these problems. 'We shall therefore establish a censorship over writers of such stories,' wrote Plato, 'and shall desire mothers and nurses to tell only the authorized fictions, moulding the mind with such tales. . . .' More recently Professor Y. V. Reznik, Doctor of Educational Science, writing from the Ukraine to *The New Era*, made a persuasive plea on the same lines:

> In the Soviet Union it is accepted as self-evident that the Government must defend its citizens, young and old, not only against worthless adulterated foods, which are a peril to physical health, but also against vulgarity, pornography, Chauvinism and anti-Semitism, which have an even graver influence upon the mind and outlook of the children. This regard for the quality of children's and young people's literature . . . is one of the most important preoccupations not only of the specialist educational authorities, but also of communal and governmental organizations. This question attracts a good deal of attention from parents and the Soviet community generally. In this way harmony is achieved in the cultural activities of the family, society, and the schools, which lightens the work of the teachers and is a guarantee of success in the complex and responsible business of bringing up the rising generation.

Since then, young people's literature seems to have shared in the spasmodic and uncertain, but none the less welcome, thaw which has been observed in Soviet culture generally. *The Times* reported recently: 'When the magazine *Moskva* printed a serious article which argued that Daniel Defoe's *Robinson Crusoe* may "leave undesirable marks on the youthful consciousness" because of its emphasis upon the accumulation of things – seen in Crusoe's salving work – on locks and fences and also because he had a faithful servant, a critic was able to poke fun at this, suggesting that it would be better, perhaps, to import a Party activist and some popular masses to Crusoe's island and then to indulge in some good trade union work.'

Even thus modified, the censorship method does not recommend itself in this country. 'Children are *people*,' Anne Carroll Moore reminded us, 'with tastes infinitely more original, more varied and more to be individually regarded during the first and second decade of life when they are coming alive, than in the third or fourth when they are static or beginning to die.' Even in the field of sex she doubted the wisdom of any hard-and-fast limitation of permissible themes. 'A frank determination to know all that can happen to human beings in books or in life is quite different from a prurient curiosity. . . . I have never felt shocked to find other boys and girls similarly impelled to find out all that they can. Tragedy lies . . . not in knowing too much but rather in not knowing enough to think things through.'

Some hard things have been said in the foregoing chapters about certain books and certain tendencies, but if criticism, even condemnation, were to mean censorship, it would be better to remain silent. There must always be some bad books published: out of them, Time winnows the good. The most we should try to do is decrease the proportion of chaff, and help Time in various ways to winnow more effectively.

How to begin? There's no place to begin. Like all educational problems it's a whirling roundabout, and you jump on wherever you can. The parent says, how can she encourage a new type of book until it arrives in the shop for her to buy? The author says, how can he afford to write it till he's sure of a demand? And the publisher stands like Janus, facing both ways, often benevolent and always cautious. As there must be some order of discussion, however, let us take the chronological order and begin with the creators of the new book.

If any of my fellow-authors have done me the compliment of reading this survey they may feel disposed to agree, after studying the evidence, first, that certain themes have been so shockingly overworked that no self-respecting writer with any pretensions to originality can decently use them for the next ten years, unless he introduces a conspicuously novel treatment

(I should hate to suggest a 'ban' on anything, but how about a self-denying ordinance, to go slow on the secret passages and stolen jewels, the hidden treasure and the hooded horrors?); second, that certain other themes, so far neglected, would repay handling, and that in choosing a theme for his next book an author should consider its social value as well as its literary possibilities; thirdly, that certain themes, attitudes and fantasies, whether overworked or not (and they usually are), should be avoided as psychologically or socially undesirable. In this connection I would merely ask them to listen to the expert witnesses cited – Heaven forbid that I, a storyteller like themselves, should even appear to lay down the law. If authors would merely accept and act on these three principles, apart from any other suggestions we have discussed, they would not endanger their livelihood, yet they would go far to eliminating the grounds for adverse criticism. Of artists we can only say that they are limited in certain respects by the books they are given to illustrate and the publishers who call the tune. What they can do, unaided, to improve the standard of illustrating lies between them and their consciences. This paragraph may stand as written in the first edition. Whether by coincidence or not, its strictures no longer apply to most of our better books, but there is enough hackneyed junk still being produced to make the criticism relevant.

Publishers and editors can play a tremendous part. They can assist writers in their self-denying ordinance (we are a weak-willed, lazy lot, many of us, and need to hear the crack of the master's whip now and again) by simply turning down hackneyed plots. 'We are not taking any more twins this year,' they might remark civilly, when sending back the manuscript. Or, 'Our stables are full. So are the tumbrils – the guillotine no longer thirsts for French aristos, at least in the printing-works. We have already used our quota of whimsy animals for the next three years.' That would teach us. And it would do us no harm, provided the letter went on with suggestions for new work that we *could* do.

It is a fallacy to suppose that every good book springs spontaneously from the brain of its author. Many (like *Little Women*) have begun as a publisher's suggestion and have been undertaken with reluctance, but they have ended as first-rate stories none the less. This is very different, however, from the process of mere 'book making', when publishers for purely commercial motives rack their brains to find an idea for a series (because a series is easier to sell than a number of separate titles) and then proceed to enlist a team of contributors, some of whom are almost inevitably sub-standard but are the only writers available to fill certain gaps in the list. At its best, the midwifery of publishers and agents has brought a number of good children's stories into the world. More often, unfortunately, by encouraging unnecessary duplication, synthetic series, and superfluous sequels, it has contributed to that over-production of different titles – running now at over two thousand juvenile books per year, including the non-fiction – which is one of the biggest problems facing us.

Any voluntary restriction of output, in a difficult trade with scores of desperately competing firms, is about as hard to achieve as disarmament between the nations. One thing publishers could do now is to combine in discrediting the out-of-date practice of buying juvenile copyrights.

What writer can be expected to put his best into his work when he has to sell it outright for a sum like forty pounds? That was the figure paid by respectable, old-established firms for a story as long as this book, when I first came into the profession, and writers are still being sent offers of as little as fifty pounds – and are accepting them. Many children's books are leisure-time labours of love. Even fifty pounds is pleasant if you have a salary or are a housewife, and it is hard to blame the flattered beginner for accepting. Publishers do not expect to get the work of established writers at this price, but there are always plenty of beginners, and they can go on reprinting indefinitely, modernizing the clothes on the dust-jacket, even changing the title, without the tiresome necessity of paying royalties. It is not hard to see why so much mediocre fiction fills the shops.

This practice is not followed by those general publishers who have turned to children's stories only in the last few decades, and who, it is interesting to note, produce most of the good work. It is however, the habit of some firms with ancient and honoured names, which used to enjoy a monopoly in the old days of heavily bulked volumes and abundant colour-plates. Naturally they cling to a tradition which is so profitable, though it is no more defensible today than that other once-reputable tradition, by which the author paid for publication. That method – save when applied to learned treatises and other matter with no commercial demand – is now rightly stigmatized as fit only for shark-publishers. It has been drummed out of the trade, and it is high time the outright purchase of juvenile copyright went after it.

'This is all very interesting, all very sad,' murmurs the general reader, 'but surely it is essentially a trade matter, and nothing to do with me?'

This is another fallacy. The exploited writer has no choice but to churn out more and more books. Ideas and inspiration cannot keep up with the flow of words, there is no time for research, no incentive to write better than he needs to satisfy the man who sends the cheque. Whether the books sells two thousand or two hundred thousand copies will make no difference to him. If it is a children's classic in twenty-five years' time, it will not bring him another penny. So why bother? Outright purchase of copyright results in a mighty clutter of mediocre books – not merely by people who could write better but have neither time nor the incentive to do so, but by people whose work would always fall short of a proper publication standard. This was tacitly admitted to me by the children's editor of a famous company as recently as 1960. Did I realize, asked this warm-hearted man, that he had a number of writers dependent upon him for their daily bread, that their books were not of a quality that would 'stand a royalty', and that without the system of outright purchase 'they would never be published at all'?

The proliferation of these mediocre books naturally increases the selection-problem for us all at every stage – the bookseller

ordering and stocking, the librarian and the teacher, the private
customer, the child consumer. It also has an important economic
effect. These books – often known as 'rewards' (not so much
because any self-respecting educational authority would now
give them as prizes, but presumably because they are so reward-
ing to their publishers) – undercut the royalty-bearing kind,
not only by saving on payment to the authors but also, as close
examination usually reveals, by offering poor paper, printing,
binding, and illustrations. If customers would more often glance
at the number of pages, they might also see that they were
getting short measure. No effort is spared to produce a cut-price
article. At the same time other firms, having bought their
manuscripts cheap, prefer to spend the full normal amount with
the papermaker, printer and binder, to get a decent-looking
volume indistinguishable from the royalty-bearing books in
their own list. In these cases either the prices are the same
(doubling the profit on the non-royalty book) or a shilling or
two lower (keeping the profit margin much the same, but winning extra sales). In the latter case there is admittedly a cash
benefit to the customer, provided that the publisher has managed
to get hold of a good book, as he still sometimes can from an
innocent or desperate author, and provided also, of course, that
the customer does not mind benefiting from exploitation.

This benefit is in any case rare and in the long run illusory,
for which ever way these firms produce and price their books
the general effect of copyright-purchase is the same: many
inferior books are published which never should be, many
struggling professionals are goaded into over-production,
and the proportion of good-quality books becomes smaller.
If the total sales of children's books remain unaltered, the average book, good or bad, sells fewer copies. As smaller editions
mean higher prices, the economic effect of all this mediocrity
is to keep up costs all round. The discriminating book-buyer,
who imagines that he is unaffected by the gaudy trash he would
never dream of buying for his own children, should reflect
that the volume he chooses would be cheaper if it were one of
only a thousand new books, and not two thousand, published

every year. It is not only the author's royalty which makes his purchase more expensive than the 'reward' on the next shelf – it is the unnecessary multiplication of titles, as mentioned in an earlier chapter, due not solely but in considerable measure to this publishing practice, keeping up production costs for all.

I have brought in the general public because, as I have tried to show, this tremendous question of outright copyright purchase is not just an internal trade matter, not just an ethical one, demanding the outsider's sympathy for an exploited category of worker, but one which affects the customer's pocket in a way he seldom realizes. There is not much he can do about it, except perhaps to give a harder look at the books displayed before him and to remember some of the various factors determining price. Clearly, though, it is for the authors and publishers to get rid of a practice so debasing to literary standards, and those publishers who do not do so voluntarily must expect to meet with increasing pressure. While it is true that authors will never have, or wish to have, a closed shop in the rigid sense, they can accomplish a good deal by the pooling of information, and this was one of the primary tasks to be undertaken by the Children's Writers' Group of the Society of Authors, one of that Society's newest subsidiary organizations founded in 1963. The Group has several other admirable objects, such as the maintenance and raising of the status of children's writing generally and the promotion of contacts between children's writers throughout the world, but none has aroused more enthusiasm than its fight against outright purchase. Members can pool their experiences and compare the practices of various publishers. They know which firms 'try it on' first, but, when their plausible outright offer is rejected, discover that after all they can afford to pay a royalty.

An interesting example of this came to my notice soon after the publication of the first edition. An old-established author, whose work I had rather ungently criticized on specific grounds, discovered that we lived in adjacent counties and suggested a meeting. Any initial embarrassment was soon forgotten and a pleasant acquaintance developed. Soon I had an opportunity of introducing him to a publisher and getting him a commission he was very pleased to undertake. I was a little apologetic about the royalty-scale, which, I said, was perhaps not quite as favourable as he got from his regular publishing house, one of the oldest and proudest (and occasionally most pompous) in the country. 'Royalties?' he exclaimed. 'I have never received a royalty in my life.' I stared back at him. 'But you have had about twenty books published by—' 'Yes, but they always buy the copyright.' I was able to assure him from my certain knowledge that this was not their invariable practice. When he sent them his next manuscript he asked for a royalty agreement and got it.

The Children's Writers' Group can organize this exchange of information more systematically, so that, as time goes by, publishers will find it harder and harder to buy manuscripts from full-time writers. The inexperienced beginner may continue to provide game worth hunting, especially since the first book of a part-timer can often be a very good one, its spontaneity and freshness more than compensating for any technical deficiencies. It is hard to protect these beginners from the consequences of an unfair first contract (which may tie them to selling several further books on the same terms) because their very existence is unknown until their books appear. They do not realize, in their natural diffidence, that they are welcome to consult the Society of Authors from the moment they receive the first letter making an offer for their book and that all the resources of the Society (including legal knowledge and a bottomless fund of confidential inside information) are available to help them avoid making a bad bargain. This cannot be too widely known. It is not philanthropy. Unfair agreements harm not only the author who signs them but all other authors too, and ultimately, by perpetuating hackwork, they harm children's literature as a whole.

Once the book is published it deserves serious, expert reviewing. There is a shocking lack of this, and it is useless for editors to plead shortage of space. There was no more criticism of juvenile literature before the war: there were merely more columns of 'notices' towards Christmas time. The most important part of a book was the blurb on the inside flap of the jacket. Sorting out a pile of press-cuttings one could always see how many had been compiled from this source, without further examination of the book. Berwick Sayers was complaining in 1932 that it was poor criticism 'to say that it is "exciting," "thrilling," or that "no normal boy or girl will be able to resist it" '. Criticism, he said, 'is still in an elementary state, and there is as yet no sound system of the psychology of children's reading'. In America Miss Moore was writing: 'Informed criticism of good work and poor work is the need of our time. Without it we cannot hope for any considerable amount of distinctive, original writing . . . The absence of any body of sustained criticism . . . has naturally resulted in a series of fashions in children's books, characterized by mediocrity, condescension and lack of humour.' It was no better in Europe. 'Criticism has adopted the habit, so far as juvenile literature is concerned,' wrote Jeanne Cappe, 'of being uniformly laudatory and approving. To go by it, this literature would be always by definition good, always to be recommended, always "to be put into any hands" '.

British reviews are certainly not 'uniformly laudatory' nowadays, though editors are seldom indifferent to the sale of advertising space in the adjoining columns and some insist on the 'mentioning' of as many titles as possible, rather than full treatment of a few, perhaps because in their hearts they do not believe that children's literature can be taken seriously. That fundamental belief causes other editors to pass over a handful of juveniles to a reviewer who can string them together into a witty, if patronizing, article. In this respect the children's author is treated little worse than any other kind of author. He just has to accept the fact that modern journalism has little use for the quiet, judicial review in which the author's purpose is stated and the extent of his success measured, with the good points set against the bad. The editor does not want a summing-up, he wants a bright piece of journalism. Either an assassination or an accolade will serve his purpose, but sweet reason is unreadable.

Children's authors expect no better treatment than others. What they may justifiably complain of is the reviewing of their books by any odd eight-year-old whom the journalist has found ready to hand.

There is, of course, some thoughtful, sincere reviewing too. It is to be found in small specialized journals such as *The School Librarian*, *Junior Bookshelf*, and Mrs Fisher's individual effort, *Growing Point*, and occasionally in the bigger magazines and newspapers, such as the special twice-yearly issues of the *Times Literary Supplement* and (here and there) the *Times Educational*. We need better and fuller reviews; and not only reviews of new books but serious discussion of general matters, such as is accorded to the novel, the play, and every other form of imaginative literature. Those who doubt that serious discussion is possible should examine the steadily lengthening list of Bodley Head Monographs, in which a number of children's writers, both living and dead, are paid the compliment of full-length critical assessment.

So much for what can be done by those who are, so to speak, 'in the business'. We come now to the customer, first that fortunate buyer who is using somebody else's money – the children's librarian or the teacher, whose increasingly well-informed buying has done much to raise standards both in writing and in book-production; and then Everyman, who as parent, uncle, god-parent, or guest of the family, rushes into the bookshop sooner or later if only as the easiest escape from the Christmas present problem. He is much the same throughout the world. Jeanne Cappe watched him in Belgium:

> When I read a story to children and look at those young faces turned towards me, lit up by what they hear, I ask myself how one can go off to a booksellers' at New Year and rely, in choosing books for young people, on the multi-coloured jacket, or the more or less doubtful taste of the assistant. It is because parents buy any volume blindly, and do not dream of showing the least discrimination, that so much mediocrity and nonsense can be published. These same parents know all the brands of chocolate to indulge the greed of their little ones. On the other hand, they have no idea of what books

M

are capable of entertaining and educating them, and forming their taste.

It is not easy for the general customer to apply his weight to the economic lever. He has not the time to keep abreast of juvenile literature. But if the good books are written and published, if the reviewers give him a chance to hear of them and the local bookseller stocks them, then the least he can do is to buy them in preference to the inferior ones. Every time a book is bought with discrimination, every time a glossy oblong of trash is rejected with due contempt, a blow has been struck in the fight for better children's fiction.

'If the local bookseller stocks them . . .' If, indeed, there is a local bookseller. For, as the years go by, as the material comfort of the population rises and the educational opportunities multiply, the bookshops of Britain alarmingly diminish. Leases fall in and the bookseller cannot renew them at modern figures – his premises become a shoe-shop or a co-operative grocery store, he is driven out of the main street or even out of business entirely. That was the fate of the bookshop in the centre of Nottingham where I did my first book-buying as a schoolboy, and it can be matched in other towns throughout the kingdom. It is the same story when those grandiose schemes for 'redeveloping the city-centre' are translated into glass and concrete – the shopping precinct,which looked so gracious as a line drawing in the newspaper, with its hint of Henry Moore sculpture and a neatly furled cypress or two, emerges as a succession of the inevitable multiple stores, in which few individual traders, and certainly no bookseller, can find a home.

Let us suppose, though, that we are within reach of a book-shop. Does it contain a bookseller? By a bookseller we mean a literate, dedicated, in literary matters omniscient person who is keenly interested in supplying us with the book we want and also, if possible, tactfully bringing to our notice other books which we should want if we knew of their existence. The first objective he will achieve, even at the trouble and expense of specially ordering, if we can supply some modest clue which will assist his almost-electronic brain to identify the book. Title, author, publisher . . . He would appreciate being told all three, but he can often achieve miracles with one, and that sometimes in a garbled version. This kind of bookseller would be able to track down most of the children's stories I have recommended, unless they are out of print.

Such paragons are hard to find, but no harder, they would tell us ruefully, than the sort of staff they would like to have working under them. Let us face it. When we find a shop containing some books, we may well find behind its counter an assistant who, in her own idiom, could not care less, and would be much happier selling footwear. You ask for a certain book. She regrets (unconvincingly) that it is not in stock. She is not pleased when (as has happened more than once to me) you quickly find the book for yourself. At least, though, she can hardly prevent your buying it, whereas, if it is genuinely not in stock and you insist on ordering it, dictating accurate details, she will fight a sulky rearguard-action every inch of the way. This is not an exaggerated picture. I will not claim that it is typical – indeed, I have met far too many assistants of the other kind to believe that it is – but it is one which most regular book-buyers will recognize. The special ordering of books *is* extra trouble. Those who do not realize that every book is a different article from every other book will always consider the customer pernickety for not being satisfied to choose something else from stock. All traders like to shift the lines they have already bought. As some-one once told me, after working in the book department of a big London store during the Christmas rush: 'When anybody asked for that book of yours, after we'd sold our last copy, we had instructions to say it was "out of print".' Let us have no illusions. The ordinary adult who wishes to do his bit in raising the standards of children's fiction, by choosing books with discrimination, may have to battle against ignorance, apathy, evasion and downright falsehood to get the particular volume he wants. I say 'may'. Booksellers and their assistants, like every other human group, run through every gradation from the angelic to the infernal.

'The nation probably has the bookshops it deserves,' Mr Richard Blackwell once said in a speech to publishers. 'Most people come from homes where a book is thought to be a thick magazine. Public, academic and subscription libraries make book-buying virtually unnecessary. Whereas about £1 per head of population is spent annually on books, gambling takes £18 for every adult over eighteen years of age.' He suggested a slogan: 'Every child deserves his own bookshelf.'

An enticing thought . . . Some of us would be happy enough if every family had its own bookshelf. The depressing truth is that in so many homes the adults have neither love nor respect for books. Reading is discouraged as a waste of time, books as a waste of space and money. As a certain Mr Epstein, an American attorney, put it in a child-custody dispute, rebutting the New Jersey welfare board's criticism that there were no books in the foster-parents' house: 'Books are no longer necessary for culture. Anyone can go to the library and get his culture, without having dust-collectors in the home.'

That probably expresses the view of the majority of British people too.

To combat it is one of the most challenging cultural enterprises of this century. How far it can be done through the stories the children read depends first on us, the writers, then on the publishers and others who pass on our product stage by stage, but finally – inescapably – on the individuals making up the community.

BIBLIOGRAPHY

May Lamberton Becker. *Choosing Books for Children.* (Oxford University Press, 1937.)

Jeanne Cappe, *Contes Bleus, Livres Roses.* (Editions des Artistes, Brussels, 1940.)

F. J. Harvey Darton. *Children's Books in England: Five Centuries of Social Life.* (Cambridge University Press, 1932.)

Frank Eyre. *Twentieth Century Children's Books.* (Longmans, 1952.)

Margery Fisher. *Intent Upon Reading.* (Brockhampton, 1961.)

Roger Lancelyn Green. *Tellers of Tales* (Ward, 1946.)

Arthur Groom. *Writing for Children.* (A. and C. Black, 1929.)

Paul Hazard. *Les Livres, les Enfants, et les Hommes.* (Flammarion, Paris, 1932. Translation by Marguerite Mitchell, *Books, Children and Men*, Horn Books, Boston, 1943.)

A. J. Jenkinson. *What Do Boys and Girls Read?* (Revised edition, Methuen, 1946.)

Kathleen Lines. *Four to Fourteen.* (Cambridge, for National Book League, 1950; 2nd. ed. 1956.)

Anne Carroll Moore. *My Roads to Childhood.* (Doubleday, Doran, New York, 1939.)

G. J. H. Northcroft. *Writing for Children.* (A. and C. Black, 1935.)

George Orwell. *Inside the Whale.* (Gollancz, 1940.)

W. C. Berwick Sayers. *A Manual of Children's Libraries.* (Allen and Unwin, 1932.)

W. J. Scott. *Reading, Film and Radio Tastes of High School Boys and Girls.* (New Zealand Council for Educational Research, and Oxford University Press, 1947.)

C. A. Stott. *School Libraries: A Short Manual.* (Cambridge University Press, 1947.)

E. S. Turner. *Boys Will Be Boys.* (Michael Joseph, 1948.)

Dorothy Neal White. *About Books for Children.* (Oxford University Press, 1946.)

The One Hundred Best Books for Children (*Sunday Times*, 1958.)
The Bodley Head Monographs (various authors).
Survey of Books for Backward Readers. (U.L.P. for University of Bristol Institute of Education, 1956 and 1962.)

Index

A – Apple Pie, 35
A for the Ark, 35
Abbey stories, 108
About Books for Children, 6, 171
Abrahall, C. H., 61
Adam of the Road, 106
Adam, Ruth, 132
Adventure and Discovery, 75
Adventures of Harry Milvaine, 20
Age of Defeat, 94
Aidan and the Strollers, 106
Aiken, Joan, 52
Ainsworth, Harrison, 95
Aladdin, 127
Alcott, Louisa, 23, 135
Alice books, 17, 24, 43, 45, 127
All You've Ever Wanted, 52
Allan, Mabel Esther, 122, 151
Allen, Agnes, 56–7
Allen, J. B., 70–1
Almedingen, E. M., 51
Amalgamated Press, 71–3
American Library Association, 38
Anatole, 36
Andersen, Hans, 36, 43, 50, 61, 114
Angry Planet, 87
Annuals, 75
Another Pony for Jean, 142
Arabian Nights, 23, 42, 45, 50, 91, 114
Ardizzone, Edward, 36
Arey, J. S., 150
Argle stories, 48
Armstrong, Richard, 79, 134
Arthur, King, 51
Artzybasheff, Boris, 49
Ashton, Agnes, 106
Atkinson, M. E., 141, 145
Author, The, 10, 117, 152
Autumn Term, 122
Avalanche, 83
Avion My Uncle Flew, 62

Babar, 35–6
Bach, Sebastian, 61
Back of Time, 132
Backward Readers, Books for, 172
Bagnold, Enid, 40
Ballantyne, R. M., 17, 65, 78–9, 86, 91
Ballet Shoes, 127, 148, 150
Barne, Kitty, 60, 126, 132, 148
Barrett, Anne, 154
Baudouy, M.-A., 83
Baxter, Gillian, 145
Beano, 37, 67–8
Bear Called Paddington, 52
Becker, May Lamberton, 171
Bedknob and Broomstick, 47
Beethoven, 61
Beezer, 68–9
Belloc, H., 101
Bend in the Road, 132
Bennett, John, 106
Beowulf, 51
Berna, Paul, 83, 87, 153
Best, Herbert, 85
Bevis, 145
Bible stories, 36
Biddy Christmas, 144
Biggles, 7, 14, 80, 85, 93, 127
Biographies, 57–62
Birl, 52
Black Beauty, 141
Blackwell, Richard, 170
Blake, Sexton, 1, 66, 74–5
Blast Off at Woomera, 87
Blishen, Edward, 153
Blue Willow, 85
Blyton, Enid, 7, 22, 25, 110, 116–8
Bodley Head Monographs, 167, 172
Bolton, Ivy, 106
Bond, Michael, 52
Bonfires and Broomsticks, 47
Bonny Pit Laddie, 153

Bonzon, P.-J., 83

Books (N.B.L. journal), 26

Books, Children and Men, 4, 171

Borrowers, 48

Boucher, Alan, 105

Bowen, Marjorie, 6, 102

Bows Against the Barons, 19, 96

Boy and the Donkey, 145

Boylston, Helen Dore, 150

Boy's Own Paper, 19, 29, 65, 75–6, 108, 145

Boys Will be Boys, 75, 171

Boys' World, 67–8

Bradley, Anne, 122

Bran the Bronze-Smith, 104

Brazil, Angela, 108

Brian Wildsmith's ABC, 35

Bridge Under the Water, 106

Bright Eyes of Danger, 86

Brother Dusty-Feet, 106

Brown, Pamela, 150

Browne, Frances, 50

Buchan, John, 6, 25

Buck, Pearl, 85

Buckeridge, Anthony, 117, 122

Budden, John, 85

Budds of Paragon Row, 154

Buffalo Bill, 1, 75

Bulldozer Brown, 88, 93

Bunter, Billy, 66, 75

Bunyan, 37

Buried Day, 28

Burnett, Frances Hodgson, 127

Burrell, Kathleen, 52

Burroughs, Edgar Rice, 68, 87

Caldecott, Randolph, 35

Campbell, Marion, 105

Cannan, Joanna, 144

Capon, Paul, 99

Cappe, Jeanne, 31, 32, 46, 166–7, 171

Captain, 19

Captain Slaughterboard Drops Anchor, 35

Captives of the Moon, 87

Carlyle, 45, 101

Carol series, 150

Carroll, Lewis, 23, 24, 40, 49, 52

Catnach, James, 2

Chalet School, 108

Charnock, Joan, 56

Chatterbox, 65, 75

Chauncy, Nan, 48

Child of China, 83

Children of the Marshes, 83

Children Who Lived in a Barn, 124–5, 148

Children's Books and International Goodwill, 88

Children's Books in England, 3, 171

Children's Encyclopaedia, 18

Children's Newspaper, 18

Children's Writers' Group, 164–5

Choosing Books for Children, 171

Christmas at Timothy's, 37

Chrysalids, 87

Chums, 18, 19, 75

Church, Richard, 40, 79, 86

Cinderella, 1, 42, 52

Cloister and the Hearth, 99

Coatts, Rita, 136

Cock House at Fellsgarth, 19

Coconut Island, 85

Coke, Desmond, 117

Cole, Sir Henry, 45

Collins' Magazine, 65

Colum, Padraic, 50

Colwell, Eileen H., 7

Come In, 33

Comet, 66–8, 70

Comic Cuts, 71

Comrades for the Charter, 96

Conquered, 96

Contes Bleus Livres Roses, 31, 171

Continent in the Sky, 87

Cooper, Fenimore, 77–8

Coot Club, 139

Coral Island, 18

Corporal Corey of the R.C.M., 84

Coryell, H. V., 85

Courtney, Gwendoline, 132

Craigie, David, 87

Criss, Mildred, 62

Crompton, Richmal, 147

Cross, John Keir, 87

Cue for Treason, 97

Cumming, Primrose, 145

Curry, W. B., 117, 148

Dan Dare, 87
Dancing Star, 61
Dandy, 73
Danger on the Line, 122
Darbyshire, Shirley, 151
Darton, W. J. Harvey, 3, 46, 78, 91, 171
Dauntless Finds Her Crew, 140
Davis, A. S. K., 85
Dawlish, Peter, 89, 140, 150
Dawson, Basil, 87
Day, Thomas, 3
De Brunhoff, J. and L., 35–6
Defoe, 23, 25, 78, 82, 158
Dehn, Olive, 33
Delafield, E. M., 23, 126
De la Mare, Walter, 2, 24, 41, 52
Delius, Anthony, 53
De Monvel, Boutet, 39
Denes, Gee, 37
Denison, Muriel, 85
Deucher, Sybil, 61
Dickens, Charles, 74, 101
Discovery and Romance, 75, 145
Doctor Doolittle, 26
Dog Toby, 86
Doorly, Eleanor, 13, 60–1
Douthwaite, L. C., 89
Doyle, Sir A. Conan, 68
Drum-beats!, 48
Duchess in Disguise, 113–4
Dumas, 97
Durrell, Lawrence, 40, 86
Duvoisin, Roger, 35
Dyer, E. Brent, 108

Eager, Edward, 48
Eagle, 67–9, 76
Edmondston, C. M., 106
Education for Sanity, 148
Edwards, Monica, 144, 151
Eight for A Secret, 154
Eliot, E. C., 87
Eliot, George, 99
Elizabeth Fry, 60
Elizabethan, 65
Emil and the Detectives, 26
End of Term, 122
Enright, Elizabeth, 85

Eric, 19, 107
Escape from France, 101
Essay on Christian Education, 1
Evers, L. H., 153
Ewing, Mrs, 133
Explorers Afloat, 141
Explorers Awheel, 141
Eyre, Frank, 35–6, 40, 171

Fabulous Histories, 2
Fairchild Family, 2
Fairy Tales, various, 50
Family Book, 54
Family from One End Street, 124, 138
Family Star, 154
Far Distant Oxus, 145
Farjeon, Eleanor, 52, 62
Farm Beyond the Town, 132
Farm in Cedar Valley, 85
Faulkner, William, 94
Fearless Treasure, 48
Felicity Dances, 150
Ferry the Fearless, 104
Feud in the Factory, 134, 148
Filles et Garcons, 39
Film Fun, 66, 73–4
First Tripper, 89, 150
Fischer, Marjorie, 55
Fisher, Cyrus, 62–3
Fisher, Margery, x, 37, 87–8, 121, 167, 171
Five Farthings, 136, 148
Five Get Into Trouble, 116
Flack, Marjorie, 131
Folkard, Charles, 35
For Rupert and the King, 104
Forest, Antonia, 122
Foster, Stephen, 61
Four to Fourteen, 35, 171
France, Anatole, 24
Frey, Alexander M., 52
Friedlander, Dr Kate, 129
Froude, J. A., 57
Fu Manchu, 83, 85
Future Took Us, 48

Galdone, Paul, 36
Garnett, Eve, 124, 126, 138

Garnett, Henry, 106
Gasworks Alley Gang Goes West, 153
Gates, D., 85
Gauntlet, 48
Gay-Neck, 85
Gell, Kathleen, 33
Gem, 66, 71, 108
Gibbings, Robert, 61, 85
Gibbs, Evelyn, 30, 34
Girl, 67, 69
Girls' Fun, 117
Girl's Own Paper, 65
Girondin, 101
Glass Slipper, 52
Gleit, Maria, 83
Godwin, William, 18, 45
Golden Cloak, 99
'Golden Gorse', 141
Goldsmith, Oliver, 2, 44
Good Citizens, 62
Goodrich, Samuel, 44
Goody Two-Shoes, 2
Gorilla Hunters, 19
Graham, Eleanor, 10, 124–5, 148, 157
Grahame, Kenneth, 43, 52
Granny's Wonderful Chair, 50
Graves, Robert, 51, 96
Gray, E. J., 106
Gray, Nicholas Stuart, 52
Great Northern, 139–41
Green, Roger Lancelyn, 51, 171
Greenaway Kate, 35, 39
Greene, Graham, 14
Greentree Downs, 85
Greenwalt, Mary, 61
Grey, Judith, 113
Grice, Frederick, 106, 153
Grimm, 23, 42, 45–6, 50
Groom, Arthur, 22, 27, 88, 110, 114, 171
Growing Point, 167
Guillot, Rene, 79
Gulliver's Travels, 2, 23

Hack, Maria, 1
Hag stories, 48
Haggard, Sir Rider, 68
Haldane, J. B. S., 40

Hale, Kathleen, 36
Handel, 61
Hansard, Gillian, 93
Hari the Jungle Lad, 85
Harnett, Cynthia, 97, 105
Harris, Elsie M., 37
Harrovians, 108
Haskell, Arnold, 150
Hatcher, Jo, 153
Haydn, 61
Hazard, Paul, 4, 14, 46, 78–9, 138, 171
Heiress, 65
Hemingway, Ernest, 89
Hemming, James, 88
Henry of Agincourt, 60
Henty, G. A., 4, 14, 17, 79, 86, 91, 102
Herda, H., 50
Here We Go Round, 151
High Sang the Sword, 105
Hildick, E. W., 121, 153
Hill, The, 19, 108
His Majesty's Players, 106
Hogan, Inez, 124
Hogg, D. and H., 85
Hogg, Garry, 141
Hollis, Gertrude, 95
Holmes, Sherlock, 74, 91
Home Notes, 18
Hope-Simpson, Jacynth, 122
Horn of Merlyns, 124
Hotspur, 70
House in Turner Square, 154
House on the Cliffs, 136
Housewife, 12
Hughes, Thomas, 117
Hull, Eleanor, 51
Hull, Katharine, 145
Hundred Million Francs, 83, 153
Hurrah for Merry Sherwood, 19
Hutton, Clarke, 36
Hyde, M. L. F., 106

I Claudius, 96
I Go By Sea, I Go By Land, 85
I Had Two Ponies, 142–3
I Wanted a Pony, 142
Iliad, 5, 51
Ilin, M., 21, 55

Immortal Hour, 41
In His Little Black Waistcoat, 36
In the Reign of Terror, 101
In the Reign of the Red Cap, 101
Ingelow, Jean, 43
Innocent Eye, 17
Insect Man, 60
Inside the Whale, 107, 171
Intent Upon Reading, 37, 87, 121, 171

Jacobs, Emma, 85
Jane's Country Year, 56
Jeanette's First Term, 121
Jeanne d'Arc, 39
Jehan of the Ready Fists, 104
Jenkinson, A. J., 9, 70, 171
Jennings, 122
Jester, 18
Jim Starling, 121
Joan Goes Farming, 151
Jobson, P. A., 140
John and Mary, 124
Johns, W. E., 7, 9, 22, 80, 85, 87, 117, 146
Judith Teaches, 122, 151
Judy and Lakshmi, 85
Judy Bowman: Therapist, 151
June Grey: Fashion Student, 151
Jungle Books, 43
Jungle John, 85
Junior Bookshelf, 10, 31, 68, 78, 157, 167

Kästner, Erich, 124
Kemlo, 87
Kerin the Watcher, 104
Kiddell-Monroe, Joan, 36, 50, 52
Kilner, Dorothy, 43
King Richard's Land, 102
King Solomon's Mines, 17
Kingdom of Carbonel, 48
Kingdom of the Bulls, 99
King-Hall, Magdalen, 104, 106
King-Hall, Stephen, 65
Kingsley, Charles, 78
King's Namesake, 104
Kingston, W. H. G., 65, 78
Kipling, 14, 43, 47, 52, 108, 121

Klondike Gold, 85
Knight, Frank, 79
Knight's Fee, 106
Knock-Out, 66, 68, 71, 73
Kornitzer, Margaret, 132
Kullmann, Harry, 153

Lances and Longships, 105
Land the Ravens Found, 105
Lark in the Morn, 122
Leng, L., 131, 134
Lewis, C. Day, 2, 28, 40, 121
Lewis, C. S., 40, 87
Lewis, Elizabeth Foreman, 85
Lewis, Hilda, 47
Lewis, Lorna, 60, 134, 148, 151
Lindsay, Jack, 106
Lines, Kathleen, x, 35, 171
Lisa Goes to Russia, 56
Little Juba, 43
Little Pretty Pocket Book, 2
Little Women, 23, 29, 135, 161
Load of Unicorn, 105
Loom of Youth, 108
Lottie and Lisa, 124
Lunn, Arnold, 108
Lunt, Alice, 121, 132
Lynch, Patricia, 47, 50, 62

Mackenzie, Sir Compton, 108
McLeish, M., 31, 68
Magnet, 66, 71, 108
Magnolia Buildings, 154
Malvern, Gladys, 61
Man Who Asked Questions, 60
Man Who Came Back, 123
Manual of Children's Libraries, 9, 171
March on London, 102
Marryat, Captain, 78
Martin Rattler, 19
Marvellous Adventures, 43
Mary Stuart: Q. of Scots, 62
Masefield, John, 40, 52
Mayne, William, 14, 122, 132, 154
Mee, Arthur, 18, 20, 24
Meek, Margaret, 97
Meet the Kilburys, 119
Member for the Marsh, 122

Men of the Hills, 104
Meynell, Esther, 61
Meynell, Laurence, 106, 151
Microbe Man, 60
Miller, Wright, 56
Milne, A. A., 18, 24, 52
Mine, 65
Missing Legatee, 81
Mr Fairweather and His Family, 132
Mr Sheridan's Umbrella, 106
Mitchison, Naomi, 85, 86, 96, 105
Monsell, Helen A., 38
Moore, Anne Carroll, 30, 91, 133, 159, 166, 171
Moore, Dorothea, 101
Moore, Patrick, 87
Moorland Mousie, 141
Morris, Marcus, 67, 76
Mopsa the Fairy, 43
More Ponies for Jean, 142
Morley, F. V., 84
Morrow, H. W., 84
Moscow Has a Plan, 21, 55
Mozart, 61
Mukerji, D. G., 85
Musical Honours, 132, 148
My Roads to Childhood, 30, 171
Mystery at Witchend, 124
Myths and Legends, 50

National Book League, 26, 64
Naughtiest Girl in the School, 117
Needham, Violet, 124
Neill, A. S., 88
Nesbit, E., 17, 23, 47
New Era, 158
New Pet, 131
Newbery, John, 2
Newby, P. H., 40, 79
Nicholls, Beverley, 108
No Mistaking Corker, 144
No Ponies, 124, 142
Noble Hawks, 106
Norris, Phyllis I., 119
North Overland With Franklin, 19
Northcroft, G. J. H., 18, 29, 86, 171
Norton, Mary, 47–8
Nos Enfants, 39

O'Brien, J., 84
Odyssey, 51
O'Faolain, Eileen, 105
Old Books for the New Young, 93
Old Gang, 111
Oman, Carola, 51, 60, 96, 97, 104
One Hundred Best Books for Children, 172
Orlando, 36
Orphans of Sinitra, 83
Orwell, George, 14, 66, 69, 71–2, 74, 107–8, 111, 171
Osborne, E., 78
Ot Kauchuka do Galoshy, 45
Other Side of the Moon, 87
Otterbury Incident, 121
Out of the Silent Planet, 87
Outcast, 106
Over the Hills to Fabylon, 52
Oxenham, Elsie J., 108

Paddy's Christmas, 38
Palaces on Monday, 55
Palmer, John, 57
Pardoe, M., 48
Parley, Peter. 44
Peake, Mervyn, 35–6
Pearce, Philippa, 48
Penny Dreadful, 121
Perambulations of a Mouse, 43
Père Castor, 36
Perelandra, 87
Perfect Zoo, 52
Perkins, Lucy Fitch, 124–5
Perrault, 42, 46
Peter Duck, 141
Peter Pan, 41
Peter the Whaler, 78
Pettmann, Grace, 114
Phillips, Sir Richard, 45
Picard, Barbara Leonie, 51
Pinocchio, 26
Picture Histories, 36
Plato, 55, 158
Policeman in the Family, 151
Ponies and Poachers, 145
Pony for Jean, 142
Popular Fairy Tales, 45
Potter, Beatrix, 34, 37, 43

Power, Rhoda, 97

Powys, J. C., 79

Prelude (biog.), 61 (novel), 108

Priestley, J. B., 36

Prisoners of Saturn, 87

Prize, 65

Provensen, A. and M., 36

Puck, 18

Puck of Pook's Hill, 47, 57

Pullein-Thompson, Christine, 144

Pullein-Thompson, Diana, 142, 145, 154

Pullein-Thompson, Josephine, 143

Queensgate Mystery, 114–6

Racketty Street Gang, 153

Rackham, Arthur, 35

Radium Woman, 60

Raiders of Mars, 87

Rainbow, 18, 66–7

Rambles of a Butterfly, 43

Ransome, Arthur, 55, 126, 139–141

Raymond, Margaret, 132

Read, Sir Herbert, 17

Read, Mayne, 78

Reade, Charles, 99

Reading Tastes, etc. (W. J. Scott), 70, 171

Reason, Joyce, 104

Reason Why, 98

Reavey, George, 4

Red Eric, 18

Redlich, Monica, 126, 136, 148

Reed, Talbot Baines, 65, 107, 139

Rennie Goes Riding, 151

Retarded Readers, Books for, 25

Rewards and Fairies, 47

Rex Milligan, 122

Reznik, Y. V., 158

Rib of the Green Umbrella, 86

Richards, Frank, 75

Ring Out Bow Bells, 105

Ripley, Elizabeth, 61

Road to Miklagard, 105

Robb, John, 84

Robertson, Wilfrid, 81

Robin Hood, 21, 51, 96

Robinson Crusoe, 1, 2, 18, 78, 82, 158

Rohmer, Sax, 5

Rojankovsky, Feodor, 36

Rolling Season, 14

Romany series, 56

Ross, M. I., 85, 132

Rough Water Brown, 106

Rousseau, 3

Royalist Brothers, 104

Runaway, 106

Rupert's Annual, 14

Ruskin, 35, 49, 65

Russell, Bertrand, 46

Russell, Steven, 88

Russian Twins, 56

Sabotage at the Forge, 134

Sail Ho!, 88

St Winifred's, 19, 134

Sandford and Merton, 3

Sandham, Elizabeth, 126

Sankey, Marjorie, 85

Sarah Joins the W.R.A.F., 151

Saville, Malcolm, 10, 56, 124, 141

Sayers, W. C. Berwick, 9, 45, 69, 74, 166, 171

Scarlet Pimpernel, 100

School in Danger, 122

School Librarian, 53, 167

School Libraries: Short Manual, 171

Scott, J. M., 85, 86, 92

Scott, Sir Walter, 95, 97, 99

Scott, W. J., 70–1, 171

Secret Dog, 145

Secret Garden, 127

Secret Journey, 153

Secret of the Rocks, 106

Secret Stepmother, 132

Sedgwick, H. D., 86

Selby-Lowndes, Joan, 154

Selincourt, A. de, 60, 122

Serraillier, Ian, 13, 51, 79, 86, 152

Seven Simeons, 49

Severn, David, 48, 141, 145

Severn, Dorothy, 104

'Shalimar', 88

Shelley, 19

Shepard, E. H., 35

Sherwood, Mrs, 2
Shield Ring, 105
Ship That Flew, 47
Siege and Fall of Troy, 51
Silver Sword, 86
Simon, 104
Sindall, Marjorie A., 154
Sinister Street, 108
Sioux Arrow, 84
Six Ponies, 142
Sleigh, Barbara, 48
S.O.S. from Mars, 87
Son of the Land, 106
Songberd's Grove, 154
Soviet Literature Today, 4
Sparks Among the Stubble, 62
Spartan Twins, 124
Sperry, Armstrong, 79, 84
Splendid Journey, 84
Spurs and Bride, 95
Stables, Dr Gordon, 20
Stalky & Co., 108, 121
Stay for the Winter, 85
Stephens, James, 50
Stepmother, 132
Stepmother for Susan, 132
Stevenson, R. L., 79
Story of the Amulet, 47
Story of the Village, 56
Storyteller's Childhood, 62
Stott, C. A., 171
Strang, Herbert, 21
Strangers to Freedom, 102
Streatfeild, Noel, 48, 56, 126, 148, 150
Strong, L. A. G., 60, 102, 104, 106
Stuart, D. M., 96
Stucley, Elizabeth, 154
Students at Queen's, 150
Sturdy Rogue, 106
Style, 27–9, 49, 73–4
Suddaby, Donald, 87
Sue Barton, 150
Summer Visitors, 154
Summerhayes, R. S., 145
Sun, 66–7, 70
Sun Slower, Sun Faster, 48
Susannah of the Mounties, 85
Susannah of the Yukon, 85
Sutcliff, Rosemary, 51, 52, 97, 104–6

Swallows and Amazons, 139
Swarm in May, 122
Swift, Jonathan, 23
Swish of the Curtain, 150
Swiss Family Robinson, 18, 54, 70, 78
Swords of Iron, 104
Tail, Teddy, 18
Tale of Two Cities, 100
Tangara, 48
Tea and Hot Bombs, 148
Teaching of Art in Schools, 30
Tellers of Tales, 171
Ten Guns for Shelby, 84
Ten Saints, 62
Tenniel, Sir John, 35
Tennyson, 26
Tewari, 85
That Hideous Strength, 87
Thimble Summer, 85
Thomson, D. C., 73
Three Ponies and Shannan, 142
Threshold of the Stars, 87
Thucydides, 60
Thunder of Valmy, 99
Thwaite, Ann, 154
Tim, 36
Time and Tide, 8–9
Time Garden, 48
Times Educational Supplement, 167
Times Literary Supplement, 49, 99, 167
Titus, Eve, 36
To Worlds Unknown, 87
Tolkien, J. R. R., 40
Tom Brown's Schooldays, 23, 107, 117
Tom's Midnight Garden, 48
Trailer Trio, 85
Traveller in Time, 47
Travers, P. L., 85
Treadgold, Mary, 124, 142, 144
Treasure Island, 18
Treece, Henry, 13, 97, 104–5
Trevelyan, G. M., 100
Trevor, Meriol, 48, 87
Trimmer, Sarah, 1, 2
Tring, A. Stephen, 106, 111, 121
True to the King, 104
Trumpet and the Swan, 102
Trumpets in the West, 98
Turfcutter's Donkey, 47, 50

Turner, E. S., 75, 171
Twain, Mark, 40
Twentieth Century Children's Books, 35, 171
Twin Colts, 124
Twin Deer, 124
Twin Sisters, 126

Under Fire in Spain, 102
Under the Window, 39
Underground Alley, 132
Uttley, Alison, 18, 46–7

Vachell, H. A., 108
Valerie: Fashion Model, 151
Van der Loeff, R., 83
Verne, Jules, 19, 65, 68, 78
Viking's Dawn, 105
Viking's Sunset, 105
Vipont, Elfrida, 62, 122
Vocabulary, 26–7, 37, 49, 73
Voyage of Luna I, 87

Wagons Westward, 84
Walkey, A. S., 19, 101
Walpole, Sir Hugh, 17
Walters, Hugh, 87
War Paint, 84
Warden of the Wilds, 89
Warner, Priscilla, 144
Warrior Scarlet, 104
Water Babies, 43
Water for London, 106
Watkins, Gino, 92
Waugh, Alec, 108
We Go series, 54
Welch, Ronald, 48, 97, 101
Wells, H. G., 68, 87, 108
Westerman, P. F., 21, 102
Westward Ho!, 78
What Do Boys and Girls Read?, 9, 171
Wheeler, Opal, 61
Whinstone Drift, 134
Whistler, Rex, 36
White, Dorothy Neal, 6, 7, 50, 118, 128–9, 171

White, Eliza Orne, 132
White Eagles Over Serbia, 86
Whitehead, Frank, 26
Whitlock, Pamela, 145
Whittington, Dick, 42, 44
Widening Path, 122
Wiese, Kurt, 38
Wilde, Oscar, 49
Wildsmith, Brian, 35
Willard, Barbara, 154
William series, 147
Williams, Ursula Moray, 106
Williams-Ellis, Amabel, 50, 62
Wilson, Colin, 94
Wilson, J. G., 54
Wind in the Willows, 18, 37, 43
Wineland Venture, 105
Wish for a Pony, 142
With Kitchener in the Sudan, 19
With Roberts to Pretoria, 19
With the Allies to Pekin, 19
Wizard, 70
Wood, Lorna, 48
Woodham-Smith, Cecil, 98
Wool-Pack, 105
Woolf, Virginia, 23
Worm, 117
Worrals Down Under, 85
Writing for Children (Groom), 22, 27, 41, 44, 110, 171
Writing for Children (Northcroft), 18, 22, 86, 171
Wyndham, John, 87

Yonge, Charlotte M., 23, 126
Young Architect, 151
Young Fu of the Yangtse, 85
Young Fur Traders, 78
Young Master Carver, 106
Young Schoolmaster, 122
Young Traveller Series, 53–4, 56
Youth's Monthly Visitor, 65

Zajdler, Zoë, 50
Zinkeisen, Anna, 61